SECRETS AND SURPRISES

Senior Authors
Carl B. Smith
Virginia A. Arnold

Linguistics Consultant
Ronald Wardhaugh

Macmillan Publishing Co., Inc.
New York

Collier Macmillan Publishers
London

This work is also published in individual volumes under the titles: *Secret Spaces* and *Good News,* copyright © 1983 Macmillan Publishing Co., Inc. Parts of this work were published in earlier editions of SERIES r.

Macmillan Publishing Co., Inc.
866 Third Avenue, New York, New York 10022
Collier Macmillan Canada, Inc.

Printed in the United States of America
ISBN 0-02-131780-1
9 8 7 6 5 4 3

ACKNOWLEDGMENTS

The publisher gratefully acknowledges permission to reprint the following copyrighted material:

"The Aquanauts," adapted from *The Aquanauts* by Arthur Schaffert. Copyright © 1971 by Arthur Schaffert. By permission of Coward, McCann and Geoghegan.

"Beany and Her New Recorder," adapted from *Beany and His New Recorder* by Carol Panter. Copyright © 1972 by Carol Panter. By permission of Four Winds Press.

"The Big Pile of Dirt," adapted from *The Big Pile of Dirt* by Eleanor Clymer. Copyright © 1968 by Eleanor Clymer. By permission of Holt, Rinehart and Winston, Inc.

"The Bravest Babysitter," from *The Bravest Babysitter* by Barbara Greenberg. Copyright © 1977 by Barbara Greenberg. By permission of The Dial Press.

"The Fisherman Under the Sea," adapted from *The Fisherman Under the Sea* by Miyoko Matsutani. Copyright © 1969 by Parents' Magazine Press. By permission of Parents' Magazine Press.

"The Good Guys and the Bad Guys," from the book *The Good Guys and the Bad Guys* by Osmond Molarsky. Copyright © 1973 by Osmond Molarsky. By permission of McIntosh and Otis, Inc.

"The Hammer of Thunder," adapted from *The Hammer of Thunder* by Ann Pyk. Copyright © 1972 by Ann Pyk. By permission of G.P. Putnam's Sons.

"I never say I'm always right. . . ," from *A Rumbudgin of Nonsense* by Arnold Spilka. Copyright © 1970 by Arnold Spilka. By permission of Charles Scribner's Sons.

"The Jar of Tassai," by Grace Moon. By permission of Mrs. Francis M. Moon. Originally published in *Child Life* Magazine.

"The King Who Rained," from *The King Who Rained* by Fred Gwynne. Copyright © 1970 by Fred Gwynne. By permission of the publishers, E.P. Dutton.

"The Little Green Man," adapted from *The Little Green Man* by Mischa Damjan. Copyright © 1971 by Nord-Sud Verlag. By permission of Parents' Magazine Press.

"Max," adapted from *Max* by Rachel Isadora. Copyright © 1976 by Rachel Isadora. By permission of Macmillan Publishing Co., Inc.

"Miss Tibbett's Typewriter," adapted from *Miss Tibbett's Typewriter* by Eve Merriam. Copyright © 1966 by Eve Merriam. By permission of Alfred A. Knopf, Inc. and Eve Merriam, c/o International Creative Management.

"The Mixing Stick," from *One Hundred Plays for Children,* by Eleanore Leuser, edited by A.S. Burack, Plays, Inc., Publishers. Copyright © 1949 by Plays, Inc. This play is for reading purposes only. For permission to produce this play, write to Plays, Inc., 8 Arlington St., Boston MA 02116.

"Monsters of the Middle Ages," adapted from *Monsters of the Middle Ages* by William Wise. Copyright © 1971 by William Wise. By permission of G.P. Putnam's Sons and Curtis Brown, Ltd.

"Shells," from *I Thought I Heard the City* by Lilian Moore. Copyright © 1969 by Lilian Moore. By permission of Atheneum Publishers.

"Somersaults & Headstands," from *Stilts, Somersaults and Headstands* by Kathleen Fraser. Copyright © 1968 by Kathleen Fraser. By permission of Atheneum Publishers, and Curtis Brown, Ltd.

"Space," from the book *Poems of Earth and Space* by Claudia Lewis. Copyright © 1967 by Claudia Lewis. By permission of E.P. Dutton & Co., Inc.

"Why the Sun and the Moon Live in the Sky," by Elphinstone Dayrell and Blair Lent, Jr. Copyright © 1968 by Blair Lent, Jr. By permission of Houghton Mifflin Company.

Illustrations: Bill Anderson, Guy Billout, J. Chwast, Bill Crawford, Ray Cruz, Blair Drawson, Roberta Edelman, Jackie Geyer, Margaret Hathaway, Tom Herbert, Vladimir Fuka Hervert, Lionel Kalish, Ted Lewin, Robert LoGrippo, Bill Ogden, Jan Palmer, Achmad Pamoedjo, Jan Pyk, Ken Rinciari, Lynn Tittleman, Lynn Uhde, Charles Varner, Jon Weiman. **Photographs:** Sonja Bullaty, Bullaty-Lomeo (Ralpho Guillamette Pictures), Richard Frieman, Eva Fuka, Jane Latta, Wayne Miller (Magnum Photos), NASA, New York Dept. of Cultural Affairs, People and Places International Inc., Don Becker, L. Berman, Lewis Franck, R. Rowan, Norman Snyder, Mike Sullivan, Tomlinson, United Press International.

Contents

SECRET SPACES

Everyone has places that are special. Sometimes others know about your special places, and sometimes no one knows. Your special place may be the house where you grew up. It may be a secret room, or a special tree. You may share it with your friends, or it may be just yours.

In "Secret Spaces," you will read about a little green man who finds a very special place. You will read about a girl who has a secret place that only she and her friend know. As you read "Secret Spaces," think about the places that are special to you. Why are they special?

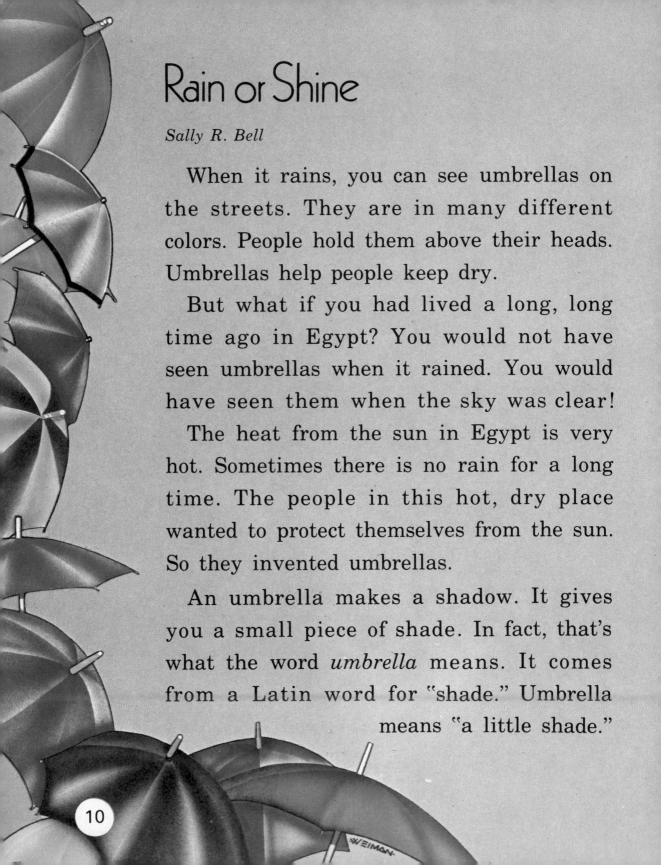

Rain or Shine

Sally R. Bell

When it rains, you can see umbrellas on the streets. They are in many different colors. People hold them above their heads. Umbrellas help people keep dry.

But what if you had lived a long, long time ago in Egypt? You would not have seen umbrellas when it rained. You would have seen them when the sky was clear!

The heat from the sun in Egypt is very hot. Sometimes there is no rain for a long time. The people in this hot, dry place wanted to protect themselves from the sun. So they invented umbrellas.

An umbrella makes a shadow. It gives you a small piece of shade. In fact, that's what the word *umbrella* means. It comes from a Latin word for "shade." Umbrella means "a little shade."

The first umbrellas were very heavy. Many of them were made of wood. None of them could fold up the way they can now.

Umbrellas were also hard to make. So for many years, most people did not have them. Only kings and queens had umbrellas. When people saw an umbrella, they knew that someone important was there.

At last, someone from a rainy place went on a trip and saw an umbrella. That person had a new thought about umbrellas. Umbrellas could protect people from the hot sun. Maybe they could protect people from the rain.

So people began to use umbrellas when it rained. But umbrellas were still hard to make. Kings and queens were still the only people who had them.

Then, about 300 years ago, people found new ways to make umbrellas. They did not use wood any more. They used metal and cloth. These umbrellas were easier to make. So more and more of them were made. Many people were then able to have umbrellas.

PARAPLUYE DANS LE TUY

These umbrellas of metal and cloth were large. One umbrella was big enough for two people to walk under it. You may see a few umbrellas as large as that today. But most of them are just the right size for one person to use.

For many years, all umbrellas were black. They did not come in the different colors you see today. You might have thought it strange to see only black umbrellas. But you would have known they were umbrellas. The shape was the same.

The shape is the one thing about umbrellas that has not changed. The shape is still the same as it was when umbrellas were invented so long ago.

The Little Green Man

Mischa Damjan

Part One
A Strange Place

Little Green Man Number 737 was sitting in his big soft chair and thinking. After a while, he felt hungry. Turning to the control panel, he pushed a button. Almost at once a plate came out. On it were four green pills. Number 737 ate them all and felt full right away.

"How easy life is," he thought, "—and how dull." He pushed another button on the control panel. His chair moved over to the window. Far down on the ground below were streets stretching as far as the eye could see.

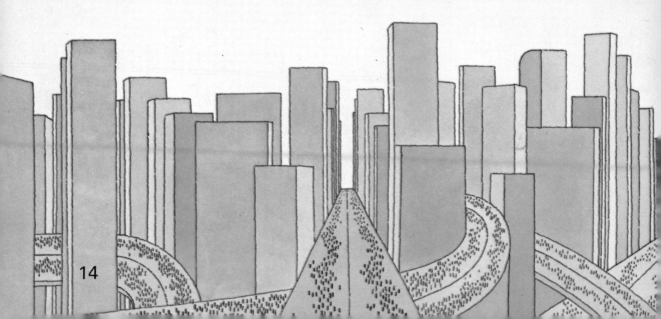

On the streets were hundreds of green people, each with two antennas. They were going every which way, but they were all standing still. Only the streets moved, carrying people here and there.

Number 737 looked over the tops of the green houses. He could see green saucers landing and taking off to fly in the green sky.

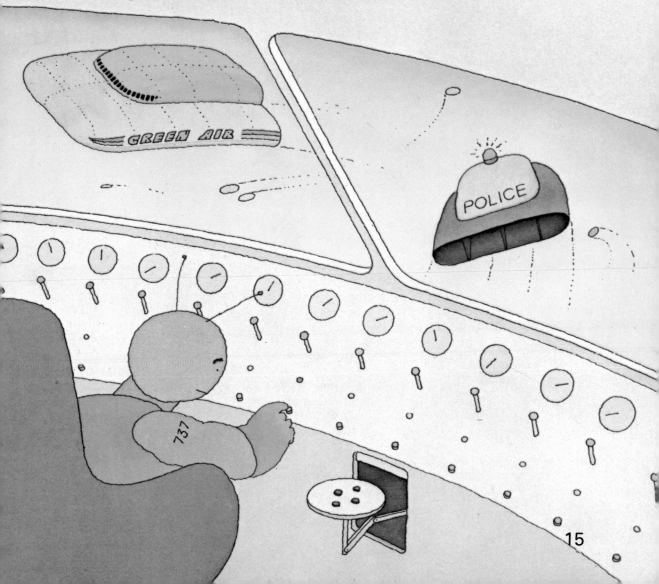

Number 737 sighed and pushed another button. The chair moved over to another window. Here he could see green children in a green playground. They were playing with a cat and mouse. The cat and mouse were machines. By pushing some buttons, the children made the cat run after the mouse. But the mouse got away.

"How dull," said Number 737. "If only the mouse would run after the cat once in a while. But the machines don't work that way. If only we had some *real* animals on this planet—even a bird. Machines are so dull. I must find some fun somewhere."

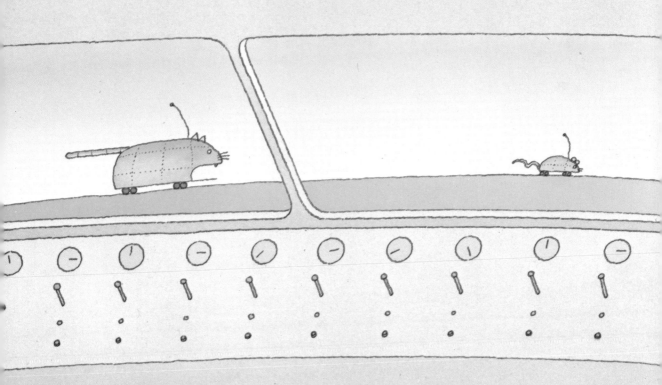

He went up to the top of his house and climbed into his flying saucer. At once it went straight up and off into space.

With great speed he flew far away from his planet, past many stars and suns. All at once, there under him lay what looked like the loveliest rug he had ever seen.

"I must land and see what that is," he said. And slowly he brought the saucer down in a very big field.

As soon as he climbed out of his ship, a strange being walked over to him. It had red hair and blue eyes, and it was wearing funny clothes.

"Hello," said the strange being. "I'm Thompson. Glad to meet you!"

"But you aren't green, and you don't have any antennas," said Number 737 with surprise. "And those animals over there," he said, pointing to a cow and two chickens. "They don't look like machines!"

Thompson laughed. "They aren't machines! The big one is my cow, Betsy, and the other two are my chickens. That's Ricky, my rooster, and Myra, my best hen." Then, taking a good look at the green man, he said, "And who are you and where did you come from?"

"I'm Number 737," he said. "I come from the Green Planet. It is many stars and suns past the Milky Way."

"Well, well," said Thompson. "You must be hungry and tired after such a long trip. Come over to the house for a bite to eat."

Number 737 was hungry. He rested in an easy chair. Thompson cooked some eggs and hot cakes and a pot of tea for his strange caller.

"What lovely pills these are!" said Number 737. "Ours are always green. What are they made of? What button did you have to push?"

Thompson laughed again. "Those aren't pills, they're eggs. And I didn't make them, Myra did. And she didn't have to push any buttons. Come, I'll show you how to eat them."

Never had 737 tasted anything so good. When he was through eating, he stretched with a sigh. He thought about the names of his new friends. Thompson . . . Betsy . . . Ricky . . . Myra . . . "I'd like a nice name, too," he said softly. "Everyone has numbers where I come from."

Thompson thought for a while. "I have it," he said. "We'll call you Zym, because that's the sound your saucer made when it came down."

"Zym . . . Zym," said Number 737. "Yes, that's a pretty name. Thank you."

It soon grew dark, and Thompson showed Zym to his room. There was a big bed with a soft down cover. Zym got in and pulled up the cover. Soon he was sound asleep. His two antennas glowed red in his sleep, because he was so happy. The animals stood around outside his window, looking in at this very strange being who had come to stay with Thompson.

Part Two
A Flower for Zym

The next morning, as the sun came up, Ricky crowed to wake everyone. Then, after a big breakfast, Zym went out to watch Thompson do his work.

He was amazed to see Thompson milking the cow. But he was even more amazed to find the egg in Myra's nest.

"What kind of animals do you have on your planet?" Thompson asked him.

"Oh, we don't have room for animals any more," Zym said. "We need all the space for machines and houses and moving roads. We do have some cats and mice, but they aren't real. They are just for playing with. You push buttons, and the cat runs after the mouse. I find it very dull."

"How sad not to have any animals," said Thompson. "But come, let's look around a bit."

22

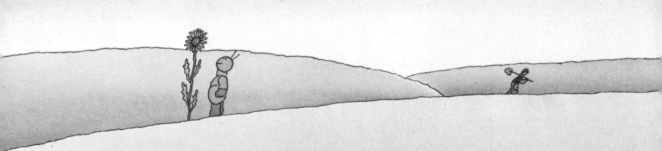

As they got to the field, Zym stopped short. "What is that? It looks like a small sun on the end of a green stick," he cried.

"It's a sunflower," said Thompson. "It's called that because it looks like the sun. It likes to turn its face to look at the sun."

"How beautiful!" said Zym with joy. "Do you mind if I just watch this wonderful flower all day?"

While Thompson went off to plow in his fields, Zym watched the sunflower.

When Thompson came back later in the afternoon, he looked very tired.

"Poor man," said Zym. "Why do you have to work so hard?"

"It's the rocks in my field," said his friend. "Every year it gets harder and harder to plow around them."

"Ho! You have been so kind to me. Now I can pay you back," said Zym. He went to his saucer and came back carrying a strange machine.

"This is a ray gun," he said to Thompson. "I'll make short work of those rocks."

He turned it on, and each time the ray hit a rock it turned the rock into fine sand.

"How can I ever thank you!" cried Thompson. "What can I give you to pay you back for your help?"

"There is only one thing I want to take home with me," said Zym. "And that's the beautiful sunflower."

Zym and Thompson were hungry after their long day. They ate a good supper that evening. Later, as they rested, Thompson asked Zym about his planet.

"Why don't you come with me and see for yourself?" said Zym. "I would like Myra to come, too, so that my friends can see how she makes her eggs."

Off they all went together, and Zym made sure he brought along his sunflower.

In no time at all they were coming in for a landing. Zym had wired ahead to his planet that he was bringing a very special friend. By the time they landed, there were hundreds of green people waiting. Thompson had never seen so much green in all his life. And the people of the Green Planet had never seen anything like Thompson. They stared at his red hair, blue eyes, and strange clothes.

Zym told them about what happened to him on Earth. He also told them how kind his friend had been to him. "Now I must show you a most wonderful thing," he said.

While everyone came around, a box was brought, filled with green straw. Myra sat on the straw. In a short time she hopped up and made a sound as if she were saying, "Look-look-look what I did! Look-look-look what I did!"

Zym held up a beautiful white egg for all to see. Thompson and Zym left the amazed people of the Green Planet to look at the egg. They went to Zym's house. In a big pot filled with green earth, they planted the sunflower. It looked lovely in the middle of all that green.

That night Thompson cooked the egg for Zym while Zym gave Thompson a supper of green pills. Thompson found the taste of the pills very strange, but they did fill him up.

While Thompson was away, the animals back home were beginning to worry. They had seen Thompson fly out of sight in the flying saucer, and they were afraid they might never see him again. All night long they watched the sky. But there was no need to worry. The next morning there was the saucer back in the field, with Zym and Thompson climbing out.

"I must return at once," said Zym. "But I will come to see you again. I really will."

Thompson threw his arms around his new friend. "Yes, yes," he said. "I will have more sunflowers for you. Also I will give you a chicken for your very own."

Then, with a loud *zym* sound, the saucer went off into space.

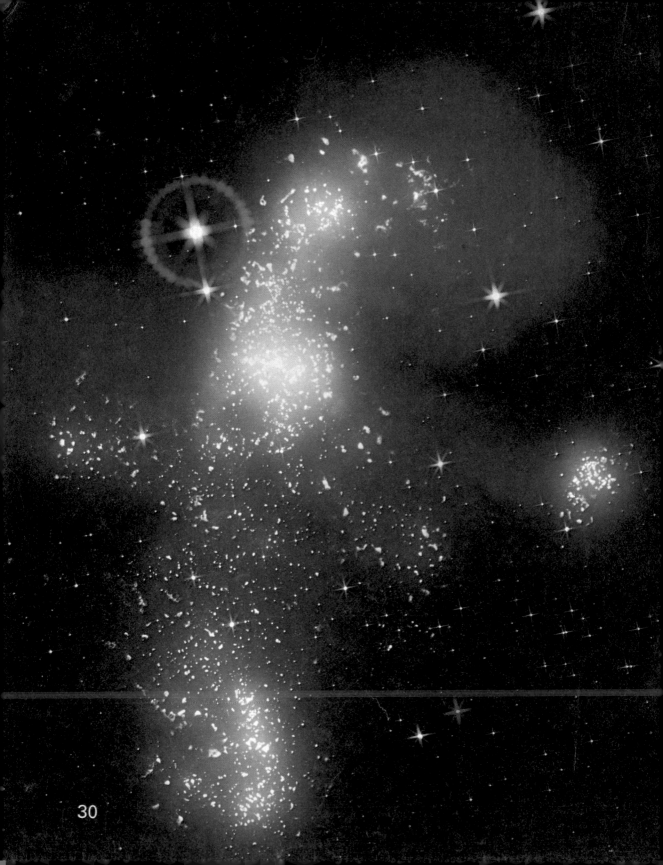

SPACE

I like the word, space,
A mighty word
With room for ace and pace and even Cape
Between its s and e;
A word suggesting air and race,
Expanse, escape,
Mystery.
In short,
Suggesting
SPACE,
That magnificent
Place.

— Claudia Lewis

The Aquanauts

Arthur Schaffert

Astronauts fly far away from the earth. They explore space and the moon. Maybe, in time, they will explore other worlds, too. Aquanauts go to the floor of the sea. They explore places just as strange and wonderful as astronauts do.

You may have seen some of the beautiful fish that swim in the ocean. If you were an aquanaut, you could go far under water. You could stay there long enough to see many unusual creatures. You would find things you never even dreamed of.

The only way you can stay under water for more than a short time is to use special gear. You must use the same kind of gear aquanauts use.

Pretend you are an aquanaut. What gear do you need? One thing you need is an air tank. The air tank gives you air to breathe under water. You wear the tank on your back. A short hose from the tank brings the air to your mouth. Before you dive, a lot of air is pumped into your tank. The tank can hold enough air for you to breathe under water for about an hour.

You also need flippers and a face mask. You wear the flippers on your feet. They help you swim under water without using your hands. The face mask covers your face. It helps you see without getting water in your eyes.

You need a heavy belt and a waterproof watch, too. The belt keeps your body under water. The watch tells you how long you have been under water. Stay less than an hour if you have only one air tank.

It's also important to have a friend with you when you dive. You and your friend can help each other under water.

Now you are ready. Your tank is full of air. The flippers are on your feet. The mask is on your face. You have a heavy belt and a waterproof watch. Your friend is ready to dive with you.

JUMP IN!

As you go down, water presses in on your body from all sides. As you go deeper, the water pressure on your body becomes greater. Now you have to breathe more air.

You breathe the air from your air tank. One end of the hose is in your mouth. At the other end, there is a valve. This valve opens and closes. It is like a door. More pressure from the water makes the valve open up more. Then you breathe in more air.

In this way, the pressure inside your body becomes the same as the pressure outside. Then you can stand the pressure of the water around you.

As soon as you are under water, you can see the bright and beautiful colors of the fish. Deeper down, everything looks blue or green. Sunlight does not go down very deep into the water. So, down deep, it is harder to see colors. It is also very cold.

There are many different creatures in the sea. Many of the fish you see will be swimming in schools. They are looking for food. Most of them are friendly.

But you might see some unusual fish. You might see a big, flat fish. It looks as if it has wings. You might see a sea horse. It swims with its head up and its tail down. It carries baby sea horses in a pocket on its front.

An octopus may come out, too. This creature hides in the rocks on the bottom of the ocean. Waving all eight arms, it will swim away from you very fast. If you follow the octopus, it will shoot out a spray of ink. While you are watching this dark cloud, the octopus swims away.

Coral grows on the ocean floor where it is not too deep or cold. You can find some beautiful coral shapes. They look like fans, branches, and flowers. These shapes are made by tiny animals inside the coral.

Your hour is almost over. It's time to go up. As you swim slowly to the top, the pressure gets lighter. The water is warmer, too. The top of the water looks like a wavy mirror. At last your head comes out. Now you can take off your face mask. You can breathe the air around you.

Aquanauts do not always have to dive to the ocean floor and come up again each day. They can live in underwater houses. Air is pumped into the houses through a long hose.

Some aquanauts have already lived and worked under water for many days. Wearing their gear, they went out of the underwater houses. They took pictures of coral. They gathered rocks from the ocean floor. They looked for signs of oil and minerals. They watched fish feed and lay their eggs. They learned a lot about life in the sea.

Much of our earth is covered by seas and oceans. We should explore this underwater world for more than just fun. There are many things we find in the sea that we can use. We can grow food in the sea. We can use seaweed to make some medicines. There is even a jelly made from seaweed that is used in making ice cream.

Scientists have also learned that many minerals can be found at the bottom of the sea. They have found oil under the ocean floor.

In the world that aquanauts explore, there are many wonderful things. Someday, everyone may share them. Maybe, in time, you will explore this world yourself.

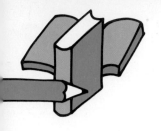

Same Sound, Different Letters

Say the words below. Listen to the vowel sounds in each word.

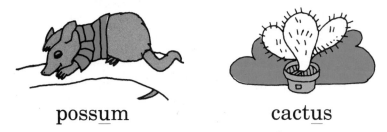

possum   cactus

These words have the same sound in the second part of the word. The sound has a special name. It is called the *schwa*. Now say these words.

woman   open   pencil   lemon

Do they have the schwa sound? Look at the letters that stand for that sound.

ACTIVITY A Say each group of words below. Listen for the schwa sound. Write the words that have the schwa sound on your paper.

1. metal   like   true   helpful
2. take   button   snow   often
3. travel   down   lemon   cure
4. most   happen   circus   bike

Say the words below. Listen for the
schwa sound.

balloon   kitten

Sometimes you hear the schwa sound in the
first part of a word. Say *balloon* again.
Sometimes you hear it in the second part.
Say *kitten* again. Now say these words.

  about   upon   broken   bottom

Do you hear the schwa sound in each
word? Look at the different letters that
stand for that sound.

ACTIVITY B Say each group of words
below. Listen for the schwa sound.
Remember it may be in the first or the
second part of a word. Write the words
that have the schwa sound on your paper.

1. dragon   rag   broken   draw
2. round   mice   above   bottom
3. across   out   aloud   ghost
4. air   upon   land   afraid

The Fisherman Under the Sea

MIYOKO MATSUTANI

Part One
The Little Turtle

Long ago there lived a good-looking young man named Taro Urashima. He was a fisherman. And he lived in a village near the sea. Each day he set out in his boat to catch fish to sell.

One day he went out to sea as always. He did not catch even one fish. Returning that night, he came upon some noisy children. They were having great fun, banging on a little turtle's shell and swinging it by the tail.

Taro was touched with pity when he saw this. He asked the children to let the turtle go. They were sorry about their treatment of the turtle. They gave the animal to Taro and ran off down the beach.

Taro now took a better look at the turtle. He was surprised to find that it was like no other turtle he had ever seen. Its shell glowed with color. At last he put the turtle down by the edge of the water. The creature quickly crawled into the waves, where it would be safe. Taro watched.

Then, just as he turned to leave, the turtle appeared again. It shook its head up and down as if to say *thank you.*

The next day Taro set out again to fish. "Let us hope that today is a lucky day for me," he said to himself. He put his net into the water.

But just then a very big turtle appeared at the edge of the boat. Bowing his head, he spoke to the amazed fisherman.

"I have come to thank you for saving the life of a small turtle," he said. "I have been told by my master, the King of the Sea, to take you down to his Dragon Palace. He wants to thank you, also. Would you be so kind as to climb on my back?"

Taro was so surprised that he did not think to say no. He jumped from his boat and quickly sat down on the turtle's back. Slowly the creature turned around. They swam down, down into the blue-green water of the sea.

All around Taro were fish of every kind and color. Strange seaweed floated in the water around him. Soon Taro and the turtle were in an underwater land of great mountains and valleys. Then, ahead of them, appeared the glowing walls of a palace. It was the Dragon Palace of the King of the Sea. The building, with its coral walls and a roof of lovely sea shells, glowed in the water.

Taro Urashima pulled in his breath with surprise. Never had the fisherman seen anything so beautiful. Servants appeared at the doorway, and he was shown into the palace. The servants showed Taro from one room to another. Each room was more beautiful than the last. Finally Taro was shown into the throne room.

There before him sat the King of the Sea. At once Taro got on his knees and bent his head before such a wonderful sight.

"Please do not bow before me," said the king kindly. "I have had you brought here so that I might thank you for saving the life of my daughter."

With this, a young girl came in and
bowed before Taro. "I was the small
turtle you saved from the children,"
she said. Her voice was like the soft
sound of far-off bells.

Taro was without words before such a beautiful girl. The princess moved like sea grass waving in the water. Her smile was as soft as the sea waves on a quiet day.

Seeing the puzzled look in Taro's eyes, she said, "I had never gone out of my home here in the Dragon Palace. I wanted to see the people who live on the land. I turned myself into a little turtle and swam to the shore of your village. But as soon as I had crawled up to the edge of the beach, I was found by those children. If you had not saved me from them, I would have come to a sad end."

Before Taro could say anything, she went on. "But I forget. You must be hungry after your long trip."

She waved her hand, and all at once there appeared a table covered with all kinds of wonderful food. In all his life, Taro had never tasted such food. The fish had a strange and wonderful taste. The cakes were as light as snow. The plates were of the best gold and silver. Also the food was brought in pots of glowing red.

Taro had hardly started to eat when the princess waved her hand again. At once, the sound of beautiful music filled the hall.

When the party was over, the princess took him by the hand. She showed him through the many rooms of the palace. After a while they came to a big window looking out upon wide fields.

It was spring. Taro could see the farmers busy planting their young rice. But as he looked the plants grew almost at once. The countryside turned from the light green of the spring to the dark green of summer. He was no sooner amazed by this when he saw that the rice plants were bent over, heavy with grain. Fall had come. Hardly was the grain picked when the snows of winter began to fall. In no more than a second, a whole year had appeared before his eyes!

Part Two
The Lacquer Box

And so the time went by for Taro in the Dragon Palace under the sea. Never had he been so happy. The beautiful princess became his beloved wife. There were servants to fill his every wish. He could not tell if it was real or just a dream.

But one day, Taro suddenly remembered his fishing boat. He remembered the joy of pulling nets filled with fish up out of the sea. He thought of his mother and his friends in the village. How he would like to see them all! How he would love to tell of his life here in the palace! He went to the princess and told her of his wish to see his village once more.

It made the princess sad to hear
Taro's wish. But she saw that he had
made up his mind. Sadly she decided
to let him go. "But take this with you,"
she said, handing him a box of the
best red lacquer. "As long as you keep
this safe, you will always be able to
come back to me." Then she stopped.
"But you must promise never to open
the box to see what is in it," she said.

Taro held his wife close. He promised
that he would never open the box.
He also promised he would return soon.
Then, with the good wishes of the
King of the Sea, he set out from the
Dragon Palace.

Once more Taro climbed on the
back of the big turtle. They began the
trip to his own land. Suddenly he could
no longer see the walls of the palace.

Through the valleys and past the mountains they went, then up, up to the top of the sea. There before him Taro saw again the houses of his village beside the sea.

He thanked the turtle for his safe trip. Then he ran up the beach to his village. But something was wrong! The mountains behind the village were still there, but the streets and houses all looked different. Taro walked through the strange streets to where his house should have been. But there was a house he had never seen before.

Going up to a villager, he asked, "Is this not the place where Taro Urashima lives?"

The man looked at him with surprise.

"Taro Urashima's house fell down many years ago," he said. "When I was a boy, my grandfather told me a story that his grandfather had told him," the villager said. "Taro Urashima went off fishing one morning and was never seen again. His boat was found, but not Taro. People thought that awful sea creatures had taken him away."

With a word of thanks, Taro turned from the villager. He walked back to the seashore. How many years had he lived in the Dragon Palace? A hundred? Two hundred? But here he was, still a young man! He was suddenly very lonely. His eyes fell on the red lacquer box. Forgetting what the princess had told him, Taro took off the string that went around the box. He opened it.

White dust appeared as he opened
the box. All at once Taro became an
old man with white hair and a long
white beard.

Then, softly, from over the water, he
heard the sad voice of the princess.
"Oh, Taro, Taro, my husband, my
beloved. You promised me that you
would never open the lacquer box. It
was your life I had closed up in the
box so that you would never grow old.
Farewell, Taro. Farewell, beloved, farewell."

And then the voice of the princess
was lost. Taro, an old man, could hear
only the sound of the sea waves as
they hit the beach at his feet.

The bones of the sea
are on the shore,
shells
curled into the sand,
shells
caught in green weed hair.

All day I gather them
and there are always
more.

Shells

I take them home,
magic bones of the sea,
and when
I touch one,
then I hear
I taste
I smell the sea
again.

—Lilian Moore

57

Beany and Her New Recorder

Carol Panter

Part One

A Family of Musicians

Beany Parker was a very special kind of girl. Pomponio was a special kind of cat. Beany and Pomponio hung out together whenever they could. They took walks together and climbed trees in the woods.

There were certain things in Beany's life which cats could not share. And there were certain things in Pomponio's life which girls could not share. But Beany and Pomponio tried to share as many things as they could.

Everyone in Beany's family was a fine musician. In the afternoon, Beany's mother cooked dinner. The rest of the family went off to different corners of the house to practice their music.

Beany did her practicing in the laundry room. Pomponio went with her. Beany's instrument was a beautiful wooden **recorder.** The recorder had a mouthpiece for blowing and seven airholes. Also there was one airhole underneath which was meant just for her thumb. Beany was a good player. She knew what to do to make the right notes come out at the right time.

Pomponio hid in the laundry basket when Beany played.

One day Beany's father said, "You're becoming a good musician, Beany. I think I should look around for another recorder for you. It will be an instrument that is even better than the one you have now."

"Wow," Beany thought to herself. She practiced her music all over again.

Pomponio hid in the laundry basket again.

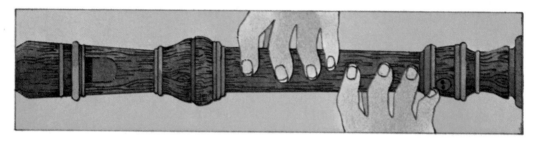

Beany's brother Sam had the best place to practice. Sam was the family keyboard player. That meant he always got the first turn at the **harpsichord**. The harpsichord looked like a small piano. But its sound was very different. When Sam struck a key with his finger, a piece of wood inside the harpsichord shot out. Then it plucked the string that he wanted. This sound was short and soft.

Sam was always playing one thing or another. Sometimes he played from printed music. Sometimes he played things which he made up himself. The harpsichord really belonged to the whole family. But Sam pretended that it belonged to him.

In the evenings and on weekends, Beany's father practiced downstairs in the mud room. The name of his instrument was the **viola da gamba**. The viola da gamba is an instrument like a cello, but with six strings. Mr. Parker always worried over them. He tuned and plucked them again and again.

"The mud room is such a cold place to practice," Beany's mother often said to her father. "You'd better wear warm clothes down there."

Beany's father wore a coat when he practiced. Often he wore a bright scarf around his neck. Mr. Parker moved the bow across the strings of the viola da gamba. He drew out the deep, sweet-singing music. The end of his bright scarf swung back and forth, keeping the beat very well.

Beany's mother called from the kitchen. "F *sharp*, Beany. That should have been an F *sharp*. And please tell your father that dinner is ready."

Beany's mother was a singer. She had a lovely, light voice. Mrs. Parker, luckily, could practice all through the day. She sang one song while she was watering the plants. She sang another song while she was driving the car. And still another one while she was working in the yard.

Besides being a singer, Beany's mother could play the recorder and the piano. She was some mother! Beany also loved her cooking.

And so did Pomponio.

After dinner, the Parkers gathered around the harpsichord with their chairs and their music stands. It was the time of day that no one wanted to miss. The Parker family played together. The beautiful sound filled the room.

Pomponio stretched out nearby. The music of Handel made him yawn.

Part Two

The Legend

One day Beany's father said, "I have a surprise for you."

Her mother and brother gathered around. And so did Pomponio. They must have known something was up. Beany's father handed her a long, thin box. "You've become a very fine recorder player, Beany," her father said. "I thought it was time to find you a very fine instrument, as I said I would."

Beany couldn't say a word. "Open it," said Mr. Parker.

Beany opened the box. She could see right away that this was a most unusual recorder.

"The recorder was made in Venice, Beany," her father told her. "And it's very, very old."

"So don't lose it," said Sam, helpfully.

"There's another thing, Beany," said Mr. Parker. "A legend from long ago comes with your recorder. The man who sold it to me asked that I pass the legend on to you."

"What is it?"

"It goes like this," Beany's father said.

> "Play ye this pipe
>
> With joy in your heart
>
> And a bird in a tree
>
> Shall join in."

"It means that if you feel happy and you take your recorder to the woods, a bird will sing along with you," said Sam.

"Wow," Beany said, "Do you think the legend is true? Do you think a bird will really sing along?"

"I would certainly expect the legend to be true," said Mr. Parker.

Beany took her beautiful new recorder and went to the woods behind her house. She picked one of her special places to sit. It was a large, flat rock near the trees.

"Come on, Pomponio," Beany called. "We'll be comfortable here."

Then Beany placed her new recorder to her mouth. She placed her fingers on the airholes. And she placed her thumb on the airhole hidden underneath. She began to play. Oh, what a wonderful sound came from this old instrument! And to think it was her very own. It belonged to *her*. Beany felt great joy in her heart. She played and played.

The woods were very quiet. Beany stopped and listened carefully. Beany did not hear one bird.

The next day Beany tried again. But this time she picked a different place to sit. It was a less comfortable place. But it was one that was near the biggest tree in the woods. The tree held the nests of many families of birds.

Beany played and played. It was the music of Bach. The sound was so lovely that it brought joy to Beany's heart. But not one bird sang.

Beany had another idea. She climbed to the other end of the woods. She took out her recorder. "Maybe birds don't like Bach," she thought. "Maybe that's why none of them sang." Beany played the music of Corelli. Again it brought joy to her heart. A rabbit stopped to listen for a while and then ran off.

But no bird sang for Beany.

After that, Beany stopped trying. But she couldn't stop thinking about her problem. Why didn't the birds sing?

The next day, the Parker family gathered with their instruments for music time. Pomponio sat on the harpsichord, carefully cleaning his paws.

"Beany doesn't seem happy tonight," said her mother.

"She's got birds on the brain," said Sam. He wanted to start playing.

Mr. Parker shook his long bow at Sam. Then he asked, "They've never sung yet, Beany?"

"Never," said Beany softly. She felt very sad.

"I wonder if we couldn't find out what's gone wrong. You should, by the legend, have joy in your heart, Beany," her father said. "Are you sure you've had it while you were playing?"

"Yes, I'm sure," Beany said, even though it was gone right now.

"Where are the birds while you're playing, Beany? What are they doing if they're not singing?" asked her mother.

"I don't know," Beany said. "I never see them. They seem to be hiding."

"Maybe they don't like you," Sam said. Again, Mr. Parker shook his bow at Sam.

But what Sam said gave Beany an idea. "What could it be that might stop a bird from singing, I wonder? It's only me, and the recorder, and Pomp-"

All of a sudden Beany took her recorder and started out of the house. Pomponio ran after her.

"Come on, Pomponio," Beany said, holding the door open. "Let's find out what's true and what isn't."

They raced off to the woods. Beany made herself comfortable on the large rock near the trees.

"Pomponio," Beany said, "will you hide in that pile of leaves over there? I'd like to try something."

Pomponio stretched each leg slowly. He seemed to be thinking.

"Pomponio," Beany said, "I think I'll play some Handel. And after that, some Scarlatti."

Beany played. Pomponio yawned when he heard the Handel. But at the first note of Scarlatti he hid deep down in the pile of leaves. Not even the tip of his tail was in sight.

"Pomponio," Beany said lovingly, "you are a most unmusical cat."

Then Beany took her new recorder and began to play again. The beautiful sound floated high up into the leafy green branches. Beany played and played. She felt great joy in her heart.

Suddenly, from a tree far in the woods, came the singing of a bird. It was a clear singing which went along with Beany and her beautiful new recorder. They filled the woods with the most lovely music.

"Mother, Daddy, Sam," Beany called into the house, "It's true! The legend is true! A bird in the woods did join in!"

"We heard it, Beany," they answered. "What wonderful music you made together!"

Pomponio climbed out of the leaves, rolled over, yawned and fell asleep.

A
Special Day

Carol Childress and Kathleen Much

Rosa and her little sister, Anita, rolled down the grassy hill. The cool grass tickled their arms. They could hear lively Mexican music coming from the other side of the hill.

The girls reached the bottom of the hill. Then they ran back to the top. Anita looked for Mama and Papa in the crowd below.

"Rosa," she said, "I don't see them."

"They're sitting near the stage," said Rosa. "Mama wanted to see the dancers from Mexico City. They have come just for the Mexican Independence Day show."

"We learned about independence in school," said Anita. "It means that a country is free. No other country tells it what to do."

"America is a free country," said Rosa. "So is Mexico. Texas was a free country for ten years. Now it is part of the United States of America. Once it was part of Mexico."

Anita asked, "If we live in Texas, why do we go to the Mexican Independence Day show?"

"Because our family came to Texas from Mexico a long time ago," said Rosa. "We're lucky. We have *three* Independence Days. We have one for Texas, one for America, and one for Mexico."

"This one is a lot of fun," said Anita. "I like the parties and the singing and the dancing. But most of all, I like the parade."

"Oh yes!" said Rosa. "Riding on a float in the parade today was fun. But the best part was wearing Grandmother's beautiful dress."

"When I'm nine, I'll get to wear the dress and ride on a float, won't I?" asked Anita.

Rosa nodded. Then she found their grandfather in the crowd. "Let's find our seats," he said. "It's time for the show."

As the stage lights went on, everyone cheered. There on the stage were two volcanoes. There, too, were the dancers dressed in costumes worn by Mexican Indians many, many years ago. At the end of the dance, sparks flew from the tops of the volcanoes. Drums beat loudly. Then a cloud floated up from the volcanoes to the evening sky. Everyone clapped.

They clapped again when the Queen of Independence Day came on stage. She began to give out the prizes. There was a prize for the best dancer. There was a prize for the best float in the parade. Then it was time to give the prize for the most beautiful costume in the parade.

"I am pleased to give this prize," said the queen, "to Rosa Hernandez. Her costume, like mine, was made like those worn when Mexico won its independence."

Rosa went up to the stage as everyone clapped. The queen handed her the prize.

"Where did you get your costume?" the queen asked.

Rosa smiled. "From my grandmother," she said. "She wore it when she was nine years old. Now that I'm nine, I can wear it. My sister, Anita, will wear it when she is nine."

"Congratulations, Rosa," said the queen.

"Thank you," said Rosa.

"Please thank your family, too," said the queen. "Thank them for taking care of your beautiful costume. It helps us remember the country from which our families came."

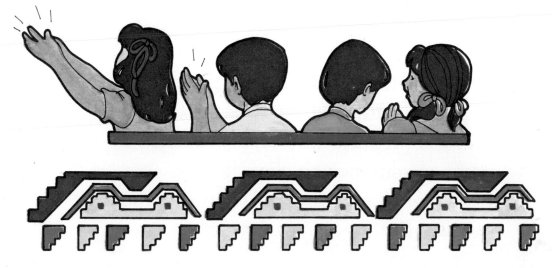

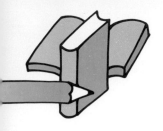

As Quiet as a Mouse

Sometimes you may want to tell about something in a new way. One way is to tell how it is like something else. Read these sentences.

> Harry is as quiet as a mouse.
> This rock looks like an egg.

Each of these sentences tells how two different things are like one another. The first sentence tells how Harry and a mouse are alike. The second sentence tells how a rock and an egg are alike. The sentences use the words *like* and *as* to tell how two different things can be alike.

ACTIVITY A   Read each set of sentences. Choose the sentence that tells how two different things are like one another. Write that sentence on your paper.

1. Isabel has many plants in her room. Isabel's room is like a jungle.

2. Allen swims like a fish.
   Allen can swim very fast.

3. Mindy sings as well as a bird.
   Mindy sings very well.

4. Mr. Perez has white socks.
   Mr. Perez has socks as white as snow.

ACTIVITY B Write each sentence part
on your paper. Then write the missing
words that show how two different
things are alike.

1. Alice's hands felt ___ .
   a. like ice
   b. very cold
   Alice's hands felt like ice.

2. Dick's dog looks ___ .
   a. like a pony
   b. furry

3. The frosting on the cake looked ___ .
   a. beautiful
   b. like real flowers

4. Tina's dress is ___ .
   a. as bright as the sun
   b. red and yellow

The Summer House Secret

Hettie Jones

Part One

Something Strange

The rain had stopped. Now only the stream and drip-drip of the trees could be heard in the warm afternoon. Kate sat in the living room, reading her letter from Alice Smith again.

"Go on outdoors, Kate. The sun's out," Aunt Isabel called from the kitchen.

Kate didn't move. *Strange things sure do happen in the city,* she read. *Last night our house was broken into, and some papers were moved around in Daddy's office. The police came! Can you imagine coming home and finding your front door broken? I sure hope our house at Shadow Lake is okay. Maybe you'd better check for us.*

"Kate Gordon!" Aunt Isabel shouted. "Out!"

Kate jumped up and ran outside, pushing the letter into her pocket. "Nothing strange ever happens here at Shadow Lake," she sighed, walking slowly along beside the stream.

A mile down, the stream ran into Shadow Lake, which gave its name to the town where Kate lived. She liked Shadow Lake in the summer, when people came from the city. But in winter, it was dull. Her only fun was making up stories like the one about the lion she saw in the woods. The lion was really Mrs. Rico's cat.

Kate went on around the lake until she came to a sign that said SMITH. Not far away, she could see some people getting Lake Road ready for summer. The countryside was nearly ready, too, Kate noticed. The colors of the leaves and flowers were even more beautiful after the rain.

Alice had written that her family would be at the lake in four weeks. Kate walked up the path to the Smith's house. "I wish Alice were here right now," she thought. "We could have so much fun."

The big house stood quiet and closed, as if it were sleeping. Kate looked at it carefully. Then she walked up to the front door. "Everything looks all right to me," she said to herself. "But I wish I could check inside, too."

Kate walked back down the path and sat on a stone bench near the house. Taking out Alice's letter, she read again: *Four more weeks and then— just you and me and the old s.p.—remember?*

How could Kate forget? The letters *s.p.* stood for "secret passageway!" It was in the Smith's house, and it went all the way from the cellar to Alice's room on the second floor. Every summer, Kate and Alice would hide there when they wanted to get away from Alice's little brother. It was their special place.

"Four more weeks," Kate said aloud, looking at the house. Then she noticed that one of the cellar windows was open a crack. She ran over and opened it all the way. "Now I can check inside, too," she thought. "I'll even be able to check the passageway!"

Kate looked around at the bench, the path, the field of flowers and waving grass. She felt as if she were the only one around for miles. Should she climb in?

Suddenly, a loud sound came from over by Lake Road. Was that the people who were working there—or was it thunder? "If it rains, I'll be better off inside," Kate thought. "Besides, Alice *did* ask me to check."

Another boom came from the lake. She turned back to the open window and quickly crawled through it.

Inside, Kate counted the stones along the cellar wall. She pushed hard on the third one she touched. With a dull, scraping sound, a door swung open. Then Kate tiptoed up the stairs of the secret passageway.

At the second floor, the stairs opened into a room with a tiny window. Kate pushed on the inside wall. Another small secret door banged open, and she crawled through it into Alice's room.

White sheets covered the bed, table, and chairs. Kate went out into the hall and looked down at the first floor. Everything in the living room was covered, too. Next to the living room was Mr. Smith's workshop.

Through the open door, she saw his drawing table, piled high with papers and tools. Mr. Smith was an architect. He sometimes worked there during the winter or sent his helpers to use the workshop. Kate often saw their cars in front of the house.

Kate walked through the rest of the house, looking in every room. She was so busy looking that she didn't hear the car until it stopped in front of the house. Quickly, she ran back to Alice's room and looked out the window. "Oh dear," she breathed. "Someone's here!"

A man got out of a blue car. "Mr. Smith must have sent an architect," Kate thought. The man walked up to the front door.

Her heart racing, Kate jumped away from the window. What if he had seen her? He would think she was snooping around. Alice had asked her to check the house, but maybe the man would be angry anyway. She had to get away!

But how? She could hide in the secret passageway until he left, but what if he stayed for a long time? Mama would worry if she didn't get home before dark. She *must* get away. She really couldn't stay hidden for very long.

A loud noise made Kate jump. What was the man doing? Quietly, she crawled out into the hall. She lay on the floor, staring down at the workshop. The light over the table had been turned on. Mr. Smith's tools were all over the floor. While she watched, the man picked up one paper after another. He looked at each one and threw it down angrily.

Kate was so amazed that for a second she couldn't think. Why was he acting so strange? Then she remembered Alice's letter: *Last night our house was broken into, and some papers were moved around in Daddy's office . . .*

"Mr. Smith didn't send that man!" Kate thought suddenly. "He must be the person Alice wrote about in her letter!"

Suddenly, Kate's heart was pounding, and she felt really scared. She crawled back through Alice's room to the secret passageway and ran down the stairs.

When she got to the cellar, she could still hear things falling in Mr. Smith's workshop. Quickly she climbed out the window and fell onto the wet grass.

In the twilight, the field of flowers looked gray. "Oh, goodness, it's late!" Kate thought. Then she ran as fast as she could, past the stone bench and out to the road.

Part Two

A Chase in the Dark

"Don't worry, Winifred, she'll be along," Aunt Isabel was saying to Kate's mother.

"But Isabel, Kate's always home long before this. It's almost dark!"

Outside, their dog began barking. The women ran to the door. Kate came running up the path, out of breath.

"Where have you been?" asked her mother.

"Whatever happened?" Aunt Isabel asked.

Kate could hardly talk. "A man . . . in the Smith's house . . . a robber."

"Kate, you know Mr. Smith often sends people to his workshop," Aunt Isabel said.

Kate jumped up. "No, he was throwing Mr. Smith's papers around. It sounds crazy, but I know he's not an architect! He's the person who broke into their house in the city. I just *know* it!"

"What are you talking about?" her mother laughed.

Kate told them about Alice's letter. Aunt Isabel still looked puzzled. "Kate, how could you see the workshop? Those windows are way over your head."

It was a while before Kate answered. "I went into the house through the secret passageway," she said at last.

Kate's mother stared. "Secret passageway? But why?"

"Alice asked me to check the house for her family. I checked outside. Then I wanted to check inside, too. The cellar window was open," Kate answered. "But then the man came. I got really scared watching him throw Mr. Smith's papers on the floor." Kate turned to her aunt. "It must be important! In the city, the police came to their house."

Aunt Isabel looked at Kate. There could be some truth to this story.

"Winifred, where are the car keys?" she asked in an excited voice.

"Isabel, do you really think we should go?" Kate's mother asked.

"We *must*," said Aunt Isabel, and that decided it. All three of them ran to the car and jumped in. Kate was excited. At last something was happening in Shadow Lake!

As they bounced along the dark road that led to the Smith's house, Kate heard a car starting up. "He's leaving!" she shouted. Suddenly, the blue car came out of the drive and went down Lake Road.

"That's him! Let's chase him, Aunt Isabel."

Aunt Isabel put on the bright headlights.
When the man saw that they were following him,
he began to speed.

Kate's mother saw the signs first. "Isabel,
watch out!" she called. Ahead, a police car's red
light swung around. A truck blocked the road
where the highway people were still working.
Unable to pass the truck, the blue car stopped
suddenly. Aunt Isabel brought their car to a stop
a few feet away.

Officer Greenly came over to them.
"Ms. Howard! And Ms. Gordon—and Kate, too!
What on earth—"

Aunt Isabel was pleased to see that the man
in the blue car had not been hurt. "Officer
Greenly," she said, "make sure that man doesn't
get away!"

Officer Greenly looked puzzled. "Will you please get out and explain this?" she asked.

"Indeed we will," Aunt Isabel said. "Come on, Kate." They walked over to the blue car.

The man stared at them angrily. "Listen," he told Officer Greenly, "the whole thing happened because of these women. I was just driving along when I noticed a car following me. I thought someone wanted to rob me, so I tried to get away."

"Is this the man, Kate?" Aunt Isabel asked. "The one in the workshop?"

"Yes," answered Kate, hardly able to look at him.

Kate's mother joined them. She explained, "Kate is sure that she saw this man in Ted Smith's workshop, throwing papers around. She also knows that someone broke into Ted's city office last week."

"How could Kate see into the workshop?" asked Officer Greenly. "Those windows are high."

"That's another story," Kate's mother said. "We'll explain later. But I do think Kate is

telling the truth. He may have been after
something in the workshop."

"Well, in that case," Officer Greenly said to
the man, "may we have a look in your car?"

"No, and I won't say another word until I see
my lawyer!" yelled the man.

"That's your right," said Kate.

"Where did you learn that?" her mother
asked.

"In school," answered Kate, proudly.
Suddenly, she noticed some papers on the back
seat of the man's car. "Look," she pointed. Aunt
Isabel pressed her nose against the window.

"Those are blueprints," she said, excitedly.
"And they say 'State Building' at the top. Ted is
going to be very surprised."

"I'll say," said Officer Greenly. "Why don't you go home now. I'll take this man in and give Ted a call. We'll be at your house later."

Kate's mother smiled at her. "I'll make tea, Officer Greenly. You'll need it by then."

Kate could hardly keep her eyes open by the time Officer Greenly and Mr. Smith came later that night.

"Got here as soon as I could," Mr. Smith said. "You can't imagine how unhappy I am. That Ben Potter worked for me for two years. Then he suddenly quit three weeks ago. Awful!"

"But why did he take the blueprints?" Aunt Isabel asked.

"To copy them and try to get the State Building job himself," Mr. Smith sighed. "Might have done it, too, if you hadn't stopped him." He smiled at Kate.

"Kate," said Officer Greenly, "you never told me how you saw Potter. Those windows are—"

"My thought, too, Officer Greenly," laughed Aunt Isabel. "But she'll tell you."

Everyone looked at Kate. "Do you want a lawyer?" Kate's mother asked, smiling.

"No, Mama," Kate smiled back. Then she explained. "Alice wrote and asked me to check the house. So I went through a cellar window that was open a little bit. Then I used the secret passageway. When the man came and I saw him throwing things, I got scared and ran."

"Well, you'd better not check any more summer houses, even if people ask you to do so," Officer Greenly said. "You leave the checking to me."

Kate's mother laughed. "Right now, I think what Kate needs is some sleep."

In bed, Kate thought about how she would tell the story. "Imagine, Alice," she would say, "this is how it happened. There we were, chasing in the dark, while Potter raced at full speed down the middle of Lake Road . . . "

At that point, Kate fell asleep.

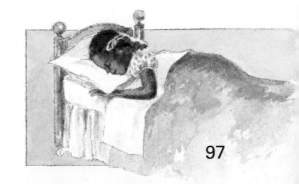

Is It Real?

Sometimes you may imagine that you are an aquanaut, a cowhand, or a scientist. It's fun to pretend what you would like to be. But it's also important to know what is real and true.

Look at this picture. It shows what is *real* and *true* about Linda.

Linda is a girl. She lives in a house in the city.

Now look at this picture. It shows what Linda *imagines* she might be.

Linda would like to be a giant. Then she would live in a big castle in the clouds.

Linda can never really be a giant. But she can imagine that she is one.

Read each set of sentences below. Choose the sentence that tells something that could *never* really happen. Write that sentence.

1. The frog sat on a log.
   The frog drove a boat on the lake.

2. "Hello!" said the dog to the cat.
   The dog barked at the cat.

3. Sandy flew over the city on a magic rug.
   Sandy saw the city from the top floor.

4. All the toys in the shop were wonderful.
   The toys danced around the shop.

5. The ghosts gave a party for the giants.
   All the children dressed up as ghosts.

6. Tom was so hungry he ate four eggs.
   Tom was so hungry he ate an elephant.

7. The tree threw its apples at us.
   We picked all the apples off the tree.

8. A fish in a red suit danced with Suzy.
   Ricky danced with Suzy.

9. Today it rained cats and dogs.
   Today it rained very hard.

MAX

Rachel Isadora

Max is a great baseball player. He can run fast, jump high, and hardly ever misses a ball. Every Saturday, he plays with his team in the park.

On Saturday mornings he walks with his sister Lisa to her dancing school. The school is on the way to the park.

One Saturday when they reach the school, Max still has lots of time before the game is to start. Lisa asks him if he wants to come inside for a while.

Max doesn't really want to, but he says OK. Soon the class begins. He gets a chair and sits near the door to watch.

The teacher invites Max to join the class, but he must take off his sneakers first. He stretches at the *barre*. He tries to do the split, and the *pas de chat*. He is having fun.

Just as the class lines up to do leaps across the floor, Lisa points to the clock. It is time for Max to leave.

Max doesn't want to miss the leaps. He waits and takes his turn. Then he must go. He leaps all the way to the park.

103

He is late. Everybody is waiting.

He goes up to bat.

Strike one!

He tries again. Strike two!

And then . . . a home run!

Now Max has a new way to warm up
for the game on Saturdays. He goes to
dancing class.

THE HAMMER OF THUNDER

Ann Pyk

Long ago, in the far, far North, there were two kingdoms in the sky. One was the home of the gods, the other the home of the giants. The gods and the giants were not friends. The greedy giants made the gods afraid. And the giants were afraid of the magic of the gods.

In the land of gods, there were all kinds of gods. There were gods of fun and tricks. There were beautiful gods, kind gods, wise ones, and strong ones. But in the land of giants, there were only big, greedy giants.

The strongest of all the gods was Thor, the god of thunder. And the biggest and greediest of all giants was Thrym. Thor had a magic hammer. He carried it wherever he went, making thunder with it throughout the sky. His hammer made him stronger than Thrym. With it he kept the kingdom of the gods safe from the giants.

The gods and the giants were almost always angry with each other. Their fights were terrible and many. But all had been quiet for a while, until one morning...

Thor got up and found his hammer was gone. He gave an angry roar as he ran to find the god of fun and tricks.

"Loki, did you take my hammer?" he cried.

"I did not," answered Loki. "My tricks are made for playing on giants, not gods."

"Who then could have taken my hammer?" cried Thor. "Our kingdom is not safe. The giants will come and take our houses, our goats, and our gold. Oh, where's my magic hammer?"

"Let's ask Freya," said Loki. "Maybe she knows where it is."

And so they ran to Freya.

"Freya, did you see my magic hammer?" asked Thor.

She shook her head. The beautiful Freya did not know where it was.

"What shall we do?" cried Thor. "Without the hammer the giants will come and take our home."

"Loki, take my coat of feathers," said Freya, "and fly down to the land of the giants. They must have taken the hammer."

"Good idea!" said Loki. "I will find those giants and get the hammer. Don't worry."

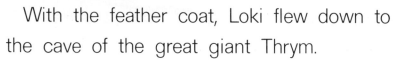

With the feather coat, Loki flew down to the cave of the great giant Thrym.

Loki landed at the mouth of the cave. He found Thrym combing a horse.

"That horse once belonged to the kingdom of the gods," said Loki. Thrym looked up from his work.

"Ah! It is Loki, I see," said Thrym. "And what brings you to the land of the giants?"

"The gods are angry," answered Loki. "Someone has taken Thor's magic hammer."

"Ho! Ho! I have it!" cried Thrym, laughing. "And I have put it eight miles deep in the earth."

"Return it at once!" shouted Loki.

"Am I a fool?" asked Thrym. "Oh, no. Not until you bring me the beautiful Freya to be my wife. Only then will Thor have his hammer."

"You are mad!" cried Loki. "Freya will never marry you."

"Then you will not see the hammer again," roared the giant.

At first Loki stared at the huge, laughing giant. Then he turned to leave.

The sound of Thrym's awful laugh followed Loki as he flew back to Freya and Thor.

When Freya heard that she must marry the terrible giant, she screamed. "Never! Never! I will never marry Thrym!" And her beads fell into a hundred pieces of anger as she ran away.

"I would never want our beautiful Freya to marry that terrible giant!" said Thor sadly.

"But we are lost without the hammer," said Loki.

"Yes, we are lost," said Thor. For a while no one said a word.

"Maybe Heimdall can help us," said Loki suddenly.

They called on the wise Heimdall for help.
And Heimdall gathered all the gods to think.
For nine days and nights they thought.
At last the wise Heimdall had an idea.

"Why not send Thor dressed as the beautiful Freya?" he said.

"I, the god of thunder, dressed as a bride?" cried Thor.

"Of course!" said Loki joyfully. "We will play a trick on the giant. You will be the bride. And I will dress as your bridesmaid!"

"Never!" shouted Thor. "Silly idea! Foolish!"

"But it will work. I know it will," said Loki.

"Well—we must try something," said Thor. "I must have my magic hammer. I will do it."

And so the plans were made.

Thor was dressed as a bride, with a veil to hide his angry eyes.

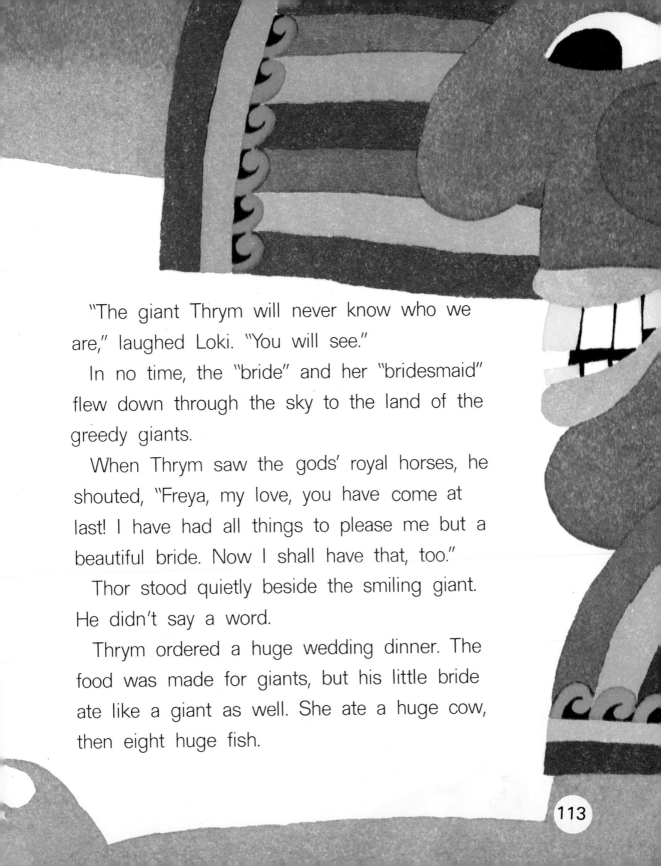

"The giant Thrym will never know who we are," laughed Loki. "You will see."

In no time, the "bride" and her "bridesmaid" flew down through the sky to the land of the greedy giants.

When Thrym saw the gods' royal horses, he shouted, "Freya, my love, you have come at last! I have had all things to please me but a beautiful bride. Now I shall have that, too."

Thor stood quietly beside the smiling giant. He didn't say a word.

Thrym ordered a huge wedding dinner. The food was made for giants, but his little bride ate like a giant as well. She ate a huge cow, then eight huge fish.

"How can my little bride eat so much?" asked Thrym.

"She fasted for nine days and nights while longing to marry you!" said the bridesmaid quickly. "That is why she eats so much."

"Ah-haaaaa!" laughed Thrym as he kissed his bride. But then he saw those angry eyes.

"How can my little bride have such angry, red eyes?" asked the giant.

Again the bridesmaid quickly said, "She could not sleep for nine days and nights. That is why her eyes are red."

The giant smiled.

Suddenly, the giant stood up. Pounding the table, he looked down at his little bride.

"BRING THE MAGIC HAMMER!" he ordered. "We will hold it in our hands as we marry. It will bring us joy forever and an end to the kingdom of the gods!"

Thor waited.

The hammer was brought to the table. Thrym stretched out his arm to take it. At the same time, Thor stretched out his arm.

The second he touched the hammer, Thor pulled off his veil. He laughed a laugh like thunder. Lightning flew from his eyes. He was strong again. He killed the giant Thrym and all the other greedy giants.

Thor had the magic hammer. Once more the kingdom of the gods was safe.

The trick had worked. And Thor and Loki flew laughing through the sky. They made thunder and lightning all the way home.

Sight and Sound

Some words sound the same when you
say them. But they have different meanings.
They also have different spellings.

Two boys ran too fast to the swings.
I would like to cut the wood.

Some words have the same sound. They
also have the same spelling. But they
have different meanings.

A new bank was built on the bank of a river.
It was hard to sleep on the hard floor.

"The King Who Rained" uses these kinds
of words in a funny way. It takes words
that sound the same and uses them with
the wrong meanings. When the words
are used this way, they are called *puns*.
After you read the story, you will work
with these kinds of words yourself.

THE KiNG WHO RaiNeD

Fred Gwynne

Daddy says there was a king
who rained for forty years.

Daddy says there are
forks in the road.

Daddy says
he has a mole
on his nose.

118

Sometimes Mommy says
she's a little horse
and needs the throat spray.

And when I give it to her,
she says I'm a little deer.

Daddy says next time he paints the house he's going to give it two coats.

Daddy says all we get in the mail are big bills.

120

My big sister's getting married and she says I can hold up her train.

DISCARD OBSOLETE

Daddy says we should live in the present.

121

Write the Right Word

Read each set of meanings below. Then read the numbered sentences. Choose the right meaning for each sentence. Then write that meaning on your paper.

Set A

A <u>fork</u> is a tool used when eating.

A <u>fork</u> is a place where a road goes in two different directions.

1. Allison used a <u>fork</u> to eat her eggs.
   ANSWER: A fork is a tool used when eating.
2. We will go right at the <u>fork</u> up ahead.
3. Please use your <u>fork</u> at dinner.

Set B

A <u>deer</u> is an animal.

<u>Dear</u> is a word that tells how much you like someone.

1. The <u>deer</u> ate some corn from my hand.
2. The little <u>deer</u> ran into the forest.
3. Tina is a very <u>dear</u> friend of mine.

Set C

To go <u>through</u> is to move from one end of something to the other.

<u>Threw</u> is a word that says you have sent something in the air.

   1. Ann <u>threw</u> the ball and broke a window.

   2. The cat jumped <u>through</u> the trap door.

Set D

A <u>bill</u> is the hard mouth of a bird.

A <u>bill</u> is a piece of paper that tells how much money to pay someone.

   1. The blue jay's <u>bill</u> is black.

   2. Rico paid the <u>bill</u> from the storekeeper.

Set E

A <u>present</u> is something that one person gives to another.

<u>Present</u> is a word that says you are somewhere at a certain time.

   1. Willie opened his birthday <u>present.</u>

   2. Kim and Ted were <u>present</u> at the church.

The Big Pile of Dirt

Part One　　　　　　　　　　　　　　*Eleanor Clymer*

No Place to Play

On our street there was an empty lot. It was small, but it was full of junk. There was an armchair with the stuffing coming out. There were boxes and tires and other things that people didn't want. And in the middle was a big pile of dirt. But I better not start telling you about that yet. First I will tell how we got started with the lot. It was like this.

See, we live in this old apartment building. There's me. My name is Mike. I'm the oldest. I have a sister, Arleen, and two brothers.

124

My brothers are twins, five years old. Their names are Billy and Sam. After school Arleen watches them, when my mother is working. I have to help her sometimes.

I have some friends who live in the building. My two best friends are Joe and Russ. We go to school together, and we're on the basketball team. After school we go somewhere and play.

That's where the trouble started. There wasn't any place to play. We couldn't all play in someone's apartment. There's no room. The apartments have too much stuff in them——beds and things.

If we played ball in the street, the little kids would run out after the ball. They could get hurt that way.

Sometimes we went up on the roof. It was nice there. You felt high up, close to the sky. You could see the tall buildings way downtown and the boats on the river. You could see white birds flying around. I liked to watch them.

But there's this lady, Mrs. Crane. Her wash got stolen once. So after that they made us get off the roof. And besides, it was no place for Billy and Sam. They might fall off. Let's face it. I couldn't get rid of them.

Then we tried to play in the side court. But Mrs. Giotto, who lived in 2A on that side, was mad at us. We laughed at her because she was fishing. I mean it. She really was.

See, it was a windy day, and she had her wash on a line outside her window. Some clothes blew down into the court. She leaned out of the window with a ball of string and a hook and let down the hook and fished up a dress. When she let down the hook again, we put an old sock on it. Mrs. Giotto looked pretty funny fishing out the window. We couldn't help laughing. So then she was mad at us and always told us to get out of the court.

Once we went down to the furnace room. It was warm there, and the furnace was like a giant with one big eye and a mouth full of fire. It was scary, but nice. But it was no use. The Super came and said, "The furnace room is no place for you. All you kids——out!"

127

We had to find a place. And it had to be a place where all of us could go. Well, right next to our house there was an empty house. No one lived in it because it wasn't safe. The house was all ready to fall down, and the doors and windows were covered with boards. One day some workers came with trucks and tore it down. We all stood around and watched.

The workers put up boards to stand on, and they climbed up and pulled pieces out of the walls. You could see inside where the bedrooms were. You could see the stairs and the kitchens.

Well, when they got through, there was nothing there but an empty lot with some bricks and old boards in it. But it didn't stay empty long. People would throw things in it——broken dishes and cans, and all the things people don't want. Or else they would come out at night and throw things there when they thought no one was looking. They put this old armchair out there, and tires and lots of other stuff.

Every day my friends and I would go and see what was there. We found some good things. I found a hammer that the workers had left. And Johnny was lucky. He found a baseball bat that looked as good as new.

This was in summer, so we played there all day every day. Joe and Russ and I made a fort out of bricks. We had to watch that the twins didn't get hurt with the broken glass and nails that were all around the lot. Arleen's friend Margie came with her little sister, and she would put things in her mouth if you didn't look out.

But still it was a pretty good place. We made a swing for the little kids out of an old tire. We hung it from some poles we drove in the ground.

And all the time we were waiting for some-one to tell us to get out, but no one did.

Part Two

How the Dirt Came to the Lot

One day when we were playing, some ladies came. They came in a car with a man. They all got out and stood looking at our lot. We watched them and heard what they said.

One lady said, "This is a mess. Look at all that broken glass and junk."

Another lady said, "That is no place for these children."

A third lady said, "How can we have a beautiful city with places like this? Mr. Mayor, you must do something."

I thought to myself, "Could that be the Mayor?" I got ready for him to run us out.

But he didn't. He just said to the ladies, "All right, I'll give orders for something to be done." Then they went away.

Joe said, "Now what? Will they make us get out?"

"No," I said, "they just want to clean it."

Arleen said, "That means we get out. I knew it."

"Well, wait and see," I said. But I was afraid she was right.

That is not what happened, though. Something different happened. One day a big truck came. It was full of dirt. Two workers got out and looked at our empty lot.

One said, "Is this the place, Mac?"

The other said, "Looks like it."

The first one said, "Are we supposed to dump the dirt here?"

The other said, "Those are the orders."

The first one said, "Then let it go."

They backed up the truck onto our lot. Then they let it go. They dumped all that dirt right in the middle of our lot. It made a noise like thunder. When the workers were finished, they went away.

Joe asked, "What's it all about?

I said, "I don't know."

We waited for something else to happen. But nothing happened. I went and stuck my hand in the dirt. It was nice and soft. It seemed like someone wanted to give us a present. I thought we might as well have some fun with it.

So I said, "Come on, kids."

Then we started playing. We climbed up the pile of dirt. I stood on top and said, "I am the President." Joe came behind me and gave me a push. I went down the dirt pile.

Then I had a great idea. I found a garbage can cover. I climbed to the top of the pile of dirt and slid down. Pretty soon all the kids were doing it.

Then we started digging. We got some pieces of board and some cans to dig with. The little kids were busy filling up old pots and dishes with dirt and making cakes. Joe, Russ, and I hadn't played in dirt for a long time, but we did it, too, just like the little kids. It was fun.

Some girls found flowers in a garbage can. They planted them in the dirt, and Margie said, "This is going to be like a park. Don't pick the flowers."

Arleen said, "If it's a park, there should be benches for people to sit on." So we made benches out of old boards. Then we pulled the old armchair up to the top of the pile. We took turns sitting in it.

I said, "Whoever is the President can sit in it." So every day another kid was President. That kid could sit in the chair and give orders to the other kids.

One day it rained. I thought, "Now it will be all mud and wash away." But it wasn't. It was like sand. The water ran through it and left it a little wet. It was better than ever. You could mold things out of it. I made a man's head and stuck an old hat on it.

Well, we kept waiting for something to happen to our pile of dirt, but nothing did, so we forgot. We just thought about it as if it was ours.

It got to be winter, and we made a snow-man on top.

Then spring came and it got warm. One day Margie started to yell, "Look! Something is growing!"

We looked, and there was green grass on one side of the dirt.

Margie said, "Don't touch it, you kids. Keep off the grass." The kids took care not to step on Margie's grass.

Then Arleen said, "We should have trees." But where could we get trees?

One day Johnny found a can of paint. He painted trees on the wall of the building next to the lot. It looked good. It was almost too good to be true, which is what my mother says sometimes.

Part Three
Mike Meets the Mayor

One day when we were playing, a car stopped and the same ladies got out. A man was with them——the same Mayor.

I said to the kids, "Hide, fast." So we hid and watched. The ladies looked at our pile of dirt. One of them got mad.

She said, "Mr. Mayor, you said you would have this place cleaned up, but nothing has been done."

The Mayor said, "Yes, I remember. I gave orders to clean it up, but someone dumped a pile of dirt in the lot. I bet someone else is still waiting for that pile of dirt."

Another lady said, "Those children are still playing in the lot. It's a dangerous place to play in."

The Mayor said, "Yes, you're right. It is dangerous. We'll have it cleaned up and a fence put around it."

Joe said, "Are they going to take away our pile of dirt?"

Arleen said, "They can't."

Two little kids started to cry.

I said, "Keep still, you kids. Let me think." The ladies were pointing at our things and talking. The Mayor kept shaking his head. I thought, "I have to do something."

Then, before I could think any more, I marched out. I felt as if someone were pushing me, only no one was. I walked right in front of them and said, "Please leave our stuff alone."

They all looked surprised. The Mayor said, "What's this? Who are you?"

I said, "I'm just one of the kids. This is our pile of dirt. We play here. Please don't take it away."

The Mayor said, "Is it all right if we look at it?"

I said, "Sure." So they went in the lot and looked at all the junk we had there.

The Mayor said, "You see, children, we want to clean this place up."

I said, "We like it this way." I was awfully scared. I thought maybe he could send me to jail for talking like that. But I had to say it. I thought, "They're going to take it away from us, and there's nothing we can do. There's no one to help us."

But all of a sudden we heard a voice. "What's wrong? Did the kids do something?"

We all looked up and there was Mrs. Giotto, leaning out of her window. She said, "Wait, I'll be right down." It didn't take her long to get down.

She said, "Those kids are not hurting anyone. You leave them alone."

I sure was surprised. She wasn't mad at us after all! The Mayor and the ladies were surprised, too.

One lady said, "But don't you see, this lot is dangerous."

Mrs. Giotto said, "No one got hurt here yet. Those kids have no place to play. You should leave them alone."

Then the Super came out. He said,
"They don't get into trouble any more.
It's a good thing for them."

Then I saw my mother coming home
from work. When she saw all the people,
she got scared. "What happened?" she asked.

Arleen said, "We're all right, Mama.
But they want to clean up our pile of dirt."

Mama said, "Clean it up? What for? It's
all right the way it is."

And suddenly I thought, "What do you
know! They're all on our side! They're all
fighting for us!"

The Mayor looked at us standing there.
Then he looked at the ladies. And then he
smiled.

He said, "You know what? I have a great
idea. We'll make a park here for the kids."

Then everyone began to smile, too, and
nod their heads. And Mrs. Giotto said, "Now
you're talking."

The Mayor said, "We'll clean it up and put in benches and swings and pipes to crawl through and things to climb on. How would you like that, children?"

We stood there and couldn't say a word. It was too sudden. But then Billy said, "What about our pile of dirt?"

The Mayor said, "Well, I don't know. It's hard to keep a pile of dirt clean. It gets all over everything."

Then I got brave and said, "We don't care. We like it." And all the other kids nodded their heads.

So the Mayor thought a while, and then he said, "I tell you what. We'll move the pile of dirt over to one side and put some new dirt on it. We'll build a little fence around it, and you can still have it. And we'll make a little pool for you. How's that?"

It was our turn to think. Then Margie said, "What about the grass on the pile?"

And Johnny said, "What about the painting on the wall?"

The **Mayor** said, "We could move the grass over, or we could give you some seeds to plant new grass. And we'll keep the painting. We could even give you more paint and you could paint the rest of the wall."

So we said all right.

Well, the next week the workers came back. They cleaned it all up. They moved the dirt into the back of the lot. They put in benches and swings, just like they said. And they put in pipes to crawl through and big stone animals you could climb on or just sit under and think, if you wanted to. They planted trees and flowers. And Margie put a little fence around her grass and even planted her own flowers.

And we painted the walls. We made trees and lions and all kinds of things.

It is a very good park, and everyone is proud of it. All the people on our street came to a party there. They take care of it and don't throw junk in it either. We sure needed that park.

But sometimes I go there by myself, early in the morning, or when it has just rained, and there aren't so many other people around. And I pretend. I pretend it's the way it used to be, just a big pile of dirt in the middle of an empty lot.

144

Spaces and Places

Spaces where I do what I like to do
Are fun to change around.
I like to play football in the house once in a while.
Sometimes I like to sleep outdoors on the ground.

I like to hang my coat on the floor
And keep my gerbil in the coat closet instead.
I like to read at the top of a tall tree.
I like to drink chocolate shakes in my bed.

I've heard my parents say
That everything has its own place.
But as for me, I always like to think of how to
    change around
        the places where I do
            what I like to do and
                find a *new*
                    use for an *old* space.

—Hilary Beckett

Aloha, Hawaii

Have you ever heard the word *aloha*? It's a word that comes from the state of Hawaii. It also says a lot about the people who live there.

The word *aloha* means many different things. It means "hello," "good-by," and "come back soon." It means "friend," "I'm happy," and "I like you," too. It's a word that the friendly Hawaiians use all the time.

Hawaii was settled by people from many lands throughout the world. When these people came to Hawaii, they brought their own languages and customs with them.

All these languages and customs make life in Hawaii very colorful. During the year, there are feasts, shows, parades, and folk dances from many lands. Hawaiians are people who enjoy each other's customs.

The climate of Hawaii is friendly, too. It is warm almost all year round. The Pacific Ocean around Hawaii keeps the climate mild. It doesn't get very cold in winter. In summer, it doesn't get very hot. At any time of the year, people can enjoy swimming, boating, fishing, and surfing.

The mild climate of Hawaii also helps many kinds of plants to grow. All over Hawaii, different flowers, fruits, vegetables, and trees grow. Many of the fruits and vegetables are sold to the rest of the United States and to the world.

Hawaii is also known for the beauty of its countryside. Everywhere, you can see green mountains, white sand beaches, waterfalls, and volcanoes. Hawaii is a chain of many islands formed by volcanoes that rose from the ocean floor. The Hawaiian Islands are really the tops of these mountains and volcanoes.

Today, many of the volcanoes are not active. But there is always the chance that one of them will become active and shoot fire and rocks into the sky.

Hawaii is the only state in the United States that is made up of islands. It is also the youngest state—our fiftieth state. Each year, many visitors come to Hawaii. They come not only from the other parts of the United States, but also from the rest of the world. They come to enjoy the friendly people, the unusual customs, the mild climate, and the beautiful land.

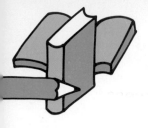

Divide the Words

Say each word below. Listen for the two parts in each word.

almost   practice   husband

Sometimes you may need to divide words like these into their parts. Look at each word. Near the middle, there are two consonant letters together. There is also a vowel letter on either side of the two consonant letters. You divide each word *between* the two consonant letters.

al/most   prac/tice   hus/band

ACTIVITY A   Look at each word below. Say it to yourself. Write the word on your paper. Then divide it into its two parts.

1. aw/ful
2. number
3. under
4. Carmen
5. garden
6. picture
7. window
8. wonder
9. order
10. barber
11. thunder
12. monkey
13. basket
14. garbage
15. bandage

16. enjoy   **17.** furnace   **18.** also

19. donkey   **20.** Gordon   **21.** princess

Now say these words. Listen for the two parts in each word.

paper   Rosa   notice

You divide these words into parts, too. Look at each word. Each word starts with a consonant letter and a vowel letter. Then there is another consonant letter with a vowel letter. The first vowel letter stands for a *long* vowel sound. You divide these words like this:

pa/per   Ro/sa   no/tice

ACTIVITY B   Look at each word below. Say it to yourself. Write the word on your paper. Then divide it into its two parts. *Remember:* The letter *y* at the end of a word can stand for a vowel sound.

1. la/zy   **2.** Peter   **3.** music

4. pony   **5.** pirate   **6.** final

7. razor   **8.** baby   **9.** tiny

SECRET SPACES

There are many things that can make a place special to you. Maybe you shared it with a very good friend. Maybe something very nice happened to you in that place.

Thinking About "Secret Spaces"

1. How did Taro Urashima find a special place for himself?
2. What special thing happened to Rosa?
3. How did Max find himself a special place?
4. What was the thing that made the empty lot special to Mike and his friends?
5. Why do you think Hawaii is a special place for so many visitors?
6. Why are your special places special for you?

GOOD NEWS

You learn things in many different ways. You learn by looking at the world around you. You learn by listening to others. You learn by reading books and by doing new things. Everything you do helps you learn about yourself and the world around you.

In "Good News," you will read about a girl who finds out that there are many ways to learn. You will read about a man who has learned to tell stories without using words. As you read, think about all the ways people learn things. In what ways do you most enjoy learning new things?

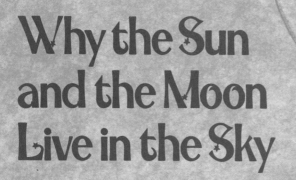

Why the Sun
and the Moon
Live in the Sky

An African folktale by *Elphinstone Dayrell*

Many years ago, the sun and the water were great friends. Both lived on the earth together. The sun very often used to visit the water. But the water never returned his visits.

At last, the sun asked the water why he never came to see him in his house. The water replied that the sun's house was not big enough. He said that if he came with his people, he would drive the sun out.

The water then said, "If you wish me to visit you, you must build a large house. But I warn you that it will have to be a very large place. I have many people. They take up a lot of room."

The sun promised to build a very large house. Soon afterwards, he returned to his wife, the moon. She greeted him with a broad smile.

The sun told the moon what he had promised the water. So the next day, he began building a large house in which to entertain his friend. When it was done, he asked the water to come and visit him.

When the water arrived, one of his people called out to the sun. She asked whether it would be safe for the water to enter. The sun answered, "Yes, tell my friend to come in."

The water then began to flow in with the fish and all the water animals. Very soon, the water was knee-deep. So he asked the sun if it was still safe. The sun again said, "Yes." So more of them came in.

Soon the water was level with the top of a person's head. Then the water said to the sun, "Do you want more of my people to come?"

The sun and the moon both answered, "Yes," not knowing any better. So the water people flowed on. Soon the sun and the moon had to perch themselves on top of the roof.

Again the water spoke to the sun. He received the same answer. So more of his people rushed in.

The water very soon overflowed the top of the roof. Then the sun and the moon were forced to go up into the sky. They have remained there ever since.

THE MIXING STICK

adapted from a play
by Eleanore Leuser

Players:

Mother Brown	Widow Post
Father Brown	Butcher
Johnny	Mrs. Goodall
Mary	Tommy
Farmer Jones	Peddler
Mrs. Jones	

Setting: A kitchen
Time: The day before Christmas

Act One

(Father and Mother Brown are sitting at a kitchen table. The table has very little food on it.)

Mother Brown: Father, it makes me sad that there is so little to eat in the house. It's the day before Christmas, too.

Father Brown: It can't be helped, Mother. It's been a hard winter. The neighbors are no better off than we are.

Mother Brown: It's the children I'm thinking about. I wish I had something hot and tasty to give them.

Father Brown: I wouldn't say no to it myself. But there . . . you can't make soup out of a pot of hot water.

(A knock is heard at the door. A happy peddler enters, carrying a big mixing stick.)

Peddler: Good day, good woman. Good day, good man. I couldn't help hearing what you said just now. If you'll give me a pot of hot water, I'll show you what can be done with it.

Mother Brown *(Rising to show him):* There's a pot half full of water on the fire, sir. But I don't understand what good that will do.

Peddler: Don't you worry, good mother. See this mixing stick. It can make the best meal you ever tasted. Just leave it all to my mixing stick and me.

Father Brown *(Watching the peddler as he starts stirring in the pot):* I've heard of strange things, but stirring hot water . . . that's the strangest!

Peddler *(To Mother Brown):* You wouldn't have a pinch of salt, would you?

Mother Brown *(Handing him some):* That's about all we do have, but you're welcome to it.

(Johnny and Mary come in, each holding an onion.)

Johnny: These onions were all we could find, Mother.

Peddler *(Rubbing his hands):* Onions, you say. That's fine, my boy. Just drop them right into the pot. They'll turn into the best meal you've ever tasted.

Mary *(Looking into the pot):* Onions and water! I don't believe it.

Peddler *(As he stirs):* It's all in the magic mixing stick, Mary, my girl. Why, when you stir with this stick, it makes a dinner fit for a king.

161

Johnny: Could we go and tell the neighbors about it, sir?

Mary: You see, it's the day before Christmas. They don't have much to eat for tomorrow. They'd be so glad to know about a mixing stick.

Peddler: Run along, both of you. Tell the neighbors they're welcome to see what I've got. You might add that if they bring a bit of what they have, I'll see to it that the mixing stick gives it a good taste.

(The children run out. The peddler stirs.)

Father Brown *(Stepping up to the pot and sniffing):* You know, Mother, I believe it's beginning to smell good already.

Mother Brown *(To Peddler):* I wish you'd tell me where to get a mixing stick like yours, sir. We need it badly around these parts.

Peddler *(Mixing and tasting):* The mixing stick is only just beginning to work. You'll really want one when it gets busy. But if you like what it makes, I'll gladly leave you this stick of mine.

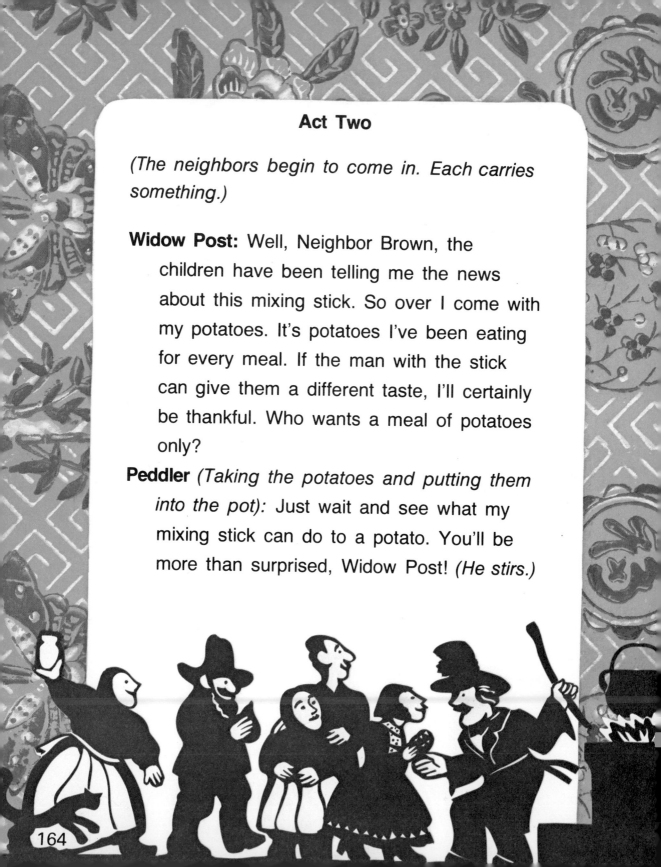

Act Two

(The neighbors begin to come in. Each carries something.)

Widow Post: Well, Neighbor Brown, the children have been telling me the news about this mixing stick. So over I come with my potatoes. It's potatoes I've been eating for every meal. If the man with the stick can give them a different taste, I'll certainly be thankful. Who wants a meal of potatoes only?

Peddler *(Taking the potatoes and putting them into the pot):* Just wait and see what my mixing stick can do to a potato. You'll be more than surprised, Widow Post! *(He stirs.)*

(Farmer Jones and Mrs. Jones enter. He is carrying some turnips. She has a jar of drippings.)

Farmer Jones: We've been hearing about the pot of water and the mixing stick. We thought that something like that is just what we need. So we've brought a few turnips to see what it does to the flavor. Sure, we've boiled turnips in water many a time. Thankful we are for them, too. But they get so uninteresting.

Mrs. Jones *(Giving a great sigh):* It's not much that we have. But here is a jar of drippings from the meat that was finished. It's been a bad year for us all . . . a bad year!

Peddler *(Taking turnips and drippings and putting them into the pot):* Fine, Farmer Jones and Mrs. Jones. I'll give them a flavor that will make your mouths water. *(He stirs and tastes.)* Um-m! It's getting delicious! This stick is wonderful!

(The butcher enters with a large bone.)

Butcher: What's all this about a magic stick that gives flavors? I'm always willing to try anything new, especially when things are so scarce. I brought this bare bone along. If you can give *that* a flavor, there's more where it came from.

Peddler *(Taking bone and dropping it into pot):* Mr. Butcher, it's amazing what a mixing stick can do with a bone. You'll scarcely believe it.

(Enter Mrs. Goodall with a sprig of parsley.)

Mrs. Goodall: The children have been telling me of a magic mixing stick and what it can do. I've only this sprig of parsley. I've been growing it in a little pot in the house. Could you turn it into something fit for a dinner?

Peddler *(Taking parsley and dropping it into the pot):* Gladly, gladly, Mrs. Goodall! *(Tasting)* Um-m, the flavor's better already. It's beyond belief what a mixing stick can do to it.

(Johnny, Mary, and Tommy enter. Tommy is carrying a few carrots.)

Tommy: It's not much that I have, sir. It's just a few carrots. We've had carrots in the morning and carrots at noon and carrots at night. Nothing else grew in our garden. It's a wonder we don't turn into carrots ourselves. But I can't get around as I ought.

Peddler *(Taking them and putting them into the pot):* Carrots, is it? Well, now, young sir, it's just the touch the mixing stick needs. They'll be wonderful for the flavor.

Mother Brown *(Looking in pot):* Why, the pot is almost full now.

Father Brown *(Sniffing):* It smells better and better.

Mrs. Jones: My mouth is beginning to water.

Peddler (*Tasting*): It's nearly ready.

Johnny (*Looking in pot):* But how will we get our onions out? I can't even see them.

Widow Post (*Looking in):* It's the same with the potatoes I brought. I don't think I'd recognize them.

Peddler (*Rubbing his hands gleefully):* Well, now, that's the trick of my mixing stick, good neighbors. You don't get just your own back. Everything is all mixed up together. It tastes better that way. There's more of it, too. One sprig of parsley doesn't make a good meal. You don't chew a bone to keep hunger away. Carrots or turnips alone make a poor supper. So put what you have together and stir with the mixing stick. When it's done, you'll find you have enough for all and a dinner that's good enough for even Christmas Day. Come, let's taste it and see.

(*Mother and Father Brown pass bowls around. The peddler fills them. All are eating and looking happy as the curtain falls.*)

Somersaults & Headstands

What are you doing?

   I'm turning a somersault.
How do you do it?

   I put my head in the grass
   and roll over like a snail.
Could you turn a wintersault?

   No, because my head would
   get cold in the snow.

Now, what are you doing?
  A headstand.
Is it like a somersault?
  Well, sort of, but you stop
  in the middle.
How do you keep from falling?
  I pretend everyone else
  is walking upside down.

                    —Kathleen Fraser

What Happens?

Read the part of a story below. The story is not finished. Something else will happen. Think how the story might end.

Anita wants to be a baseball player. Every day, she goes to the park to practice with her bat, ball, and glove. Everyone thinks she is a good player. The Bears need a new player.

How do you think the story will end? Choose one of the answers below.

The Bears will ask Anita to join the team.
Anita will stop playing baseball.

Now read the story parts on the next page. Think how each one might end. Choose an answer and write it on your paper.

Story 1 Debbie had to meet Sam in Los Angeles at eight o'clock. She took a bus that would get to Los Angeles at eight o'clock. On the way, the bus broke down. It took an hour to get it rolling again.

a. Debbie will be on time to meet Sam.

b. Debbie will be late for her meeting with Sam.

Story 2 Roberto wants to buy a rabbit. His mother tells him that he has to make the money himself. Roberto gets a job. He works every afternoon after school.

a. Roberto will buy himself a rabbit.

b. Roberto won't be able to buy a rabbit.

Story 3 Tom covered the table with a bright red tablecloth. He set blue plates and spoons at each place. Then Tom put a large bowl of popcorn in the middle of the table. On another table, there were many beautiful presents.

a. Tom will leave to go on a vacation.

b. Tom will give a birthday party for someone.

MONSTERS OF THE MIDDLE AGES
William Wise

Part One
Strange People and Places

Long before our own day, there was a time called the Middle Ages. Much of the world had not yet been discovered.

Life during the Middle Ages was very different from what it is today. It was a time when kings and queens lived in stone castles. It was a time when knights went into battle dressed in armor. Their horses wore armor, too.

Most people, though, were not kings or knights.
Some worked the land. They lived in small
villages. Some were merchants. They lived in
small towns.

During the Middle Ages most people never
went far from their homes. The roads were bad,
so it was not easy to travel. There were no cars
or planes to take people quickly from one
place to another. If people had to travel,
most of the time they rode horses or donkeys.
If they were too poor to own horses or donkeys,
they walked.

Because most people stayed near home, they
knew very little about the rest of the world.
And so they believed stories that today we know
are not true.

People in the Middle Ages believed that the
world was filled with monsters. They liked to
hear stories about strange people and animals.
These stories sound foolish now. But they did
not sound foolish to people in the Middle Ages.

One story told of a country called Abarimon. The people of Abarimon were said to have their feet turned backward.

You might think they could not get around very well with their feet turned backward. But the story said they were such fast runners that no one else could keep up with them!

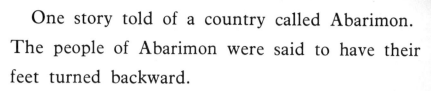

Then there were the Astomi, who were said to live in faraway India. They did not eat like other people. Rather, the Astomi fed themselves by smelling flowers!

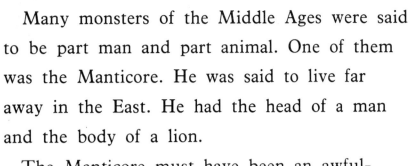

Many monsters of the Middle Ages were said to be part man and part animal. One of them was the Manticore. He was said to live far away in the East. He had the head of a man and the body of a lion.

The Manticore must have been an awful-looking monster. He had three rows of teeth and ate any animal he could catch. If he caught any people, the Manticore ate them, too.

The only nice thing about the Manticore was his voice. It was beautiful. It sounded like lovely music.

The Centaur was a strange monster. He had the head of a man and the body of a horse. His voice sounded like a horse's voice. And he could run as fast as a horse.

In some ways, though, the Centaur acted like a man. He hunted with a bow and arrows. And when he felt sad, the Centaur cried.

Still, he was not a friendly monster. Whenever people came into the deep woods where he lived, he tried to shoot them with his arrows.

Part Two
Dragons and Mermaids

Almost everyone believed in Dragons during the Middle Ages. Some Dragons had wings and could fly through the air. Others had no wings and stayed on the ground.

Some Dragons had feet, but many did not. The ones without feet looked like snakes.

A few Dragons were said to be friendly. But most were not. They breathed fire. It was said that they ate people whenever they could.

Often a dangerous Dragon lived in a cave. It might hide its gold there, for Dragons were said to love gold.

The Dragon might also kidnap a princess. It would keep the princess inside its cave until her father, the king, paid the Dragon gold to get her back.

In many stories, a young knight would put on his armor. Then he would ride off to the cave to fight the Dragon. The young knight almost always won the battle. Then he would find both the gold and the princess. Having saved the princess, he would take her home to her father. Before long, the princess would marry the knight. At the end of the story, they would become king and queen.

All during the Middle Ages, sailors liked to talk about their adventures. Sometimes they really did see strange-looking animals. We know their names today. But when the sailors got back home and told their stories, these strange-looking animals often sounded like monsters.

Many sailors said they had seen a Mermaid while at sea. The Mermaid was said to be part woman and part fish. She had long hair, which she liked to comb as she rode along the waves. Sailors believed their ship would sink if it got too close to a Mermaid.

The Mermaid may well have been just a large animal we call the sea cow. You can still find sea cows today. They are big, kind creatures that do not hurt anyone.

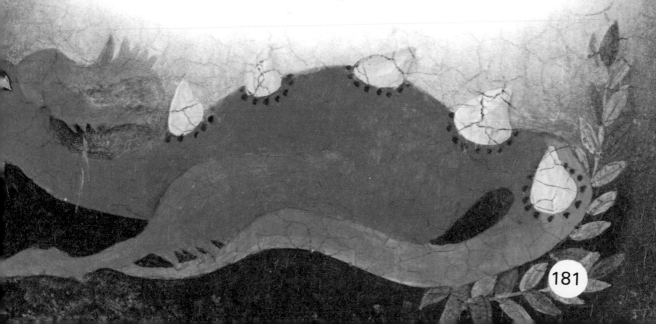

The Kraken was a sea monster of the north. In some stories, it pulled a sailor over the ship's side and carried the sailor under the waves. In other stories, the Kraken sank a whole ship, leaving just one person to tell the tale.

Few of these stories could have been true. But the Kraken *was* a real animal—a giant squid. It still can be found in the sea. It is one of the biggest creatures in the world.

One of the best-known stories told in the Middle Ages was about the Unicorn. It was a white animal with a long horn. No one could catch the Unicorn by going after it. But if a beautiful young woman were left alone in the woods, the Unicorn would come and put its head in her lap. Then it would fall asleep, and people could come and catch it.

People believed that the horn of the Unicorn had magic in it. They believed that if they ground up some of the horn and ate it, they would be safe from snakebite.

The horn of the Unicorn looked a little bit like the horn of two real animals—the rhinoceros, and the narwhal.

But the Unicorn did not look like them in other ways. It looked like a white horse, with a horn, a goat's beard, and the tail of a lion.

Today no one believes that there are any Unicorns hiding in the woods. No one believes that there are any Mermaids swimming in the sea or Dragons flying through the air.

Today we know there really are no such creatures. But for many, many years, people did believe in them—and in all the other amazing monsters of the Middle Ages.

Detail from Bathing at Asnières

The Sights and Sounds of an Artist

An artist can take us to places we've never been. What do you see in this painting? What colors did Seurat use to give us the feeling about this place? How does this painting make you feel? Why? Can you see the sunlight?

An artist can make us hear, too. What sounds do you imagine you hear as you look at this painting? Why?

Seurat. Bathing at Asnières. National Gallery, London

Georges Seurat was a French artist who lived about one hundred years ago. He painted using small dots of color. In addition to his painting, Seurat did scientific experiments with sunlight. He found that light from the sun can be split into several colors, as in the rainbow.

A SPECIAL KIND OF HELP

Laurence Swinburne

Part One

The Newcomer

Nobody wanted to sit by Rosie. It wasn't because she was new in school. It was because Rosie seemed to know all the answers. And she would always try to help the other kids, even when they didn't want any help.

Rosie's only friend was Angie. But Angie was in another class. Rosie really didn't know why she didn't have more friends. She liked to learn, and she really liked to help other people learn.

One day a new girl came to Rosie's class. "I see your name is Laura Jenkins," said Mrs. Rogers.

"That's so, ma'am," said the girl, "but my folks call me Laurie."

The kids in the class didn't quite know what to make of Laurie. Her ways were different. Some of the kids laughed at her. Others stayed away from her.

Rosie knew how she felt. She had felt that way, too, when she first came to this new school.

One day Rosie asked Laurie to eat lunch with her. The two girls talked all through lunch. Rosie learned a lot about the newcomer.

"I know the others think I'm funny," said Laurie. "I don't talk like them. And I don't know the answers to all the questions the teacher asks. But I've been living in the hills. People don't go to school much there."

"Aren't there any schools in the hills?" asked Rosie.

"There are," said Laurie. "But Daddy didn't like to send us too much. Most times we didn't have shoes or the right clothes. Daddy's come to the city to get work and try to change his luck," she said.

"Those kids don't know everything," said Rosie. "Don't worry about them."

"I wish I could talk like them," said Laurie. "And I wish I could say the answers sometimes."

"I'll help you," said Rosie. She was excited. At last she could help someone.

She introduced Laurie to Angie. Angie and Rosie began to help Laurie after school every day.

Laurie started to do better in school, but not too much better. She had a hard time giving answers to Mrs. Rogers' questions.

"Maybe I can't learn," said Laurie.

"Yes, you can," said Rosie. "It just takes time, that's all. You'll get better, just you wait and see." But deep down Angie and Rosie really thought that Laurie would never learn. They didn't think she would ever catch up.

One day the teacher told everyone that all the third-grade classes would go on a trip to Pioneer State Park. "We will go by boat up the river," she explained. "It will cost you three dollars each. The trip will take place on May 15."

Everyone was very excited. There were lots of things to be done and plans to be made.

But as time passed, Laurie seemed to get sadder and sadder.

"I sure would like to go. But three dollars is just too much for Daddy to spend. I guess I can't go," she said.

"Don't say that, Laurie! You've got to go. Maybe I can get my father to give you the money," said Rosie.

"Thanks, Rosie. But we never take money from anybody," said Laurie.

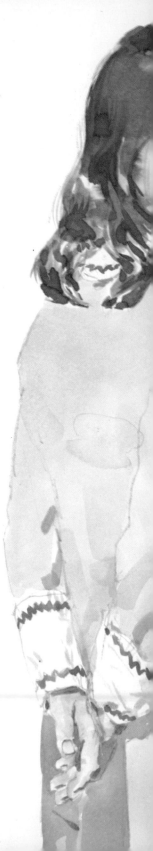

"I see what you mean," Rosie said. She was quiet for a while. But then she said, "Maybe you can earn the money."

"Earn it? You think I can?" Laurie was very excited.

Rosie and Angie got babysitting jobs for Laurie in the afternoon after school. She was good at it, too. The kids liked her because she played with them. She also collected empty bottles she found on the street and took them to the store for the money.

A week later, Laurie came to Angie and Rosie with a box of money.

"I've got it," said Laurie. "I've got the three dollars!"

Rosie counted the money. "You didn't count right," she said. "You have over four dollars!"

"Oh, I never could add too well," said Laurie.

All the kids laughed. Laurie laughed,
too. But Rosie thought it was sad that her
friend didn't know how to count.

That night she told the story about
Laurie to her family. "She's a nice girl.
But she doesn't seem to be very smart.
She can't even add!" said Rosie.

"I don't know," said her mother. "She
earned her own way, didn't she? That
was a very smart thing to do. Laurie has
missed so much school. Being good at
adding doesn't mean that someone is
smart or not smart."

Part Two

May 15

The big day they had all been waiting for finally came. All the third-graders met at the school and got on the bus. They drove down to the river and got on the boat. They were all very excited. They sailed for two hours before they got to Pioneer State Park.

There was a little village at Pioneer Park. It had been fixed up in just the way the pioneers lived two hundred years before. A man took them around and explained different things. He showed them a man milking a cow in a big barn. Most of the girls and boys had never seen that before.

"I used to do that every morning," laughed Laurie. "It seems funny going on a trip just to see that."

Next they saw a woman spinning. "Why, she's making cloth just like we used to back home," cried Laurie.

And when they saw candles being made, Laurie spoke up again. "We did that a lot. I never liked it too much though." She didn't understand why the other children were so excited.

In one house a man was making a broom. "Makes me homesick to watch him do that. We used to make our brooms just like that—out of a special kind of cornstalk," explained Laurie.

All the kids were amazed at how much Laurie knew. They followed her around to hear her explain things. They listened to her more than they did to the man.

After they had gone through Pioneer Park Village, they went on a nature walk. "Stick together now," said Mrs. Rogers. "This is not like a city park. You can get lost in these woods."

Rosie ran to a beautiful flower. "Hey, look at that flower. I've never seen a flower that looks like that."

"That's mountain laurel," said Laurie. "We had a lot of that back home. I think it's pretty, too."

"What's that one over there?" Angie asked.

Laurie took a close look at it. "Why that's chicory. We made coffee out of it back home."

They saw so many things in the woods that they didn't see they were getting away from the others.

Suddenly Rosie cried, "Where are we?"

"I don't know," said Angie, "but we'd better get back."

They started back the way they thought they had come. At last Laurie said, "We're going around in circles. We went by that old tree and that stream before."

"We're lost!" cried Rosie. "We'll never get out of here!"

Laurie put her arms around her friends. "Now hush up," she said. "People will be looking for us. We can get along."

But hours went by, and no one came. They had walked a long way.

"It's getting dark. We better stop here," said Laurie. "First off we've got to get a fire going. Make a pile of dry leaves and grass."

Laurie took the string off her dress. She tied it to a stick to make a bow. Then she took a short stick and turned it around the string. The girls couldn't believe what they saw. Laurie put the sticks into the pile of leaves. She rubbed them together and soon she had a fire. The fire made everything better.

"You're great!" said Angie.

"Now all we need is a place to sleep," said Laurie. Then she showed the girls how to make a little hut with sticks. The girls sat close together inside.

"I'm so hungry," cried Angie. "I bet they're having dinner now at home."

"That's easy to fix," said Laurie. "You two see if you can find some worms. Use sticks to dig."

They did as Laurie said. As they were digging, they saw her trying to catch flying bugs. They thought she was crazy.

But she did catch a lot. Then she took a pin from her pocket and bent it. "Fish love these bugs and worms," she said. Laurie took the string from the bow. She tied the bent pin to the end of the string. "That'll make a good enough fishing line, I guess," she said.

Laurie caught two fish. They cooked them over the fire. They ate fish off large pieces of bark. They'd never had such good fish before.

But Rosie and Angie were very quiet once they finished eating. "Maybe bears will get us tonight!" cried Rosie.

Laurie laughed. "Don't bother your mind about them. Animals won't bother you if you don't bother them. Come on, Rosie, this is fun!"

The girls fell asleep right away. No one woke up all night. But when Rosie opened her eyes the next morning, she didn't know where she was. She thought she was still asleep, dreaming. Then she remembered and started to worry, "They'll never find us."

"Oh, we can find our way out. Come on! We'll follow the stream and see where it goes," said Laurie. She loved the woods. It was like being home for her.

They followed the stream. Laurie saw how scared Rosie and Angie looked. "That stream's got to go somewhere. It goes to bigger streams or to the river. If you keep on long enough, you'll find people. That's sure," she said.

Suddenly they heard voices. Rosie and Angie began to yell. "We're here! Over here! We're here!" Some people came running out of the trees. "We have been looking for you all night," said the park ranger. "We were afraid that something had happened to you."

"Sorry we put you to so much trouble," said Laurie. "We were all right. But it wasn't smart to go so far away from the class."

Then Angie and Rosie told about Laurie and all the things she had done for them. The park ranger looked at Laurie. "You're a smart girl," he said. "You know a lot about the woods."

"It's nothing much to know," said Laurie, "when you've been brought up in the woods. Folks that don't know woods though have a pretty hard time."

When they got back to school, every-one was talking about Laurie. They had her tell the story to the whole class. No one laughed this time. "I guess being good at adding doesn't show if someone is smart or not smart," said Rosie.

She and Angie had changed their minds about their new friend.

202

I never say
I'm always right

I never say I'm always right
Although I know it's true;
I never ever start a fight —
I'll punch you if you say I do.
I'm never, never, ever sad —
Just thinking of it makes me blue;
In fact, I have no faults at all,
Except for one or two.

— Arnold Spilka

Bright, Noisy Magic

Hilary Beckett

Everyone eats supper on the beach and then waits high up on a hill for the sun to set. It's the Fourth of July! As soon as night falls, colored rockets fill the sky with sparks. Higher and higher they spray and fall!

At another time and place, a big paper dragon comes down the street. It is so big, ten people have to carry it. Excited children shout and beat on drums. They greet the dragon with tiny firecrackers. Bang! It's the Chinese New Year!

Somewhere else, a boat floats by on a lake or a river after dark. People on the shore are amazed by the fire fountains that whistle high in the air! The people have come to see a fair, and the fireworks help them to celebrate.

People all over the world love the bright, noisy magic of fireworks. They celebrate special days with rockets zipping, firecrackers popping, fire fountains whistling, and pinwheels turning and glowing in the sky. Beautiful colors explode and burst in the air! Reds, greens, blues, and yellows! What a fantastic sight!

Fireworks have been around for about a thousand years. But where did they come from? The Chinese people may have invented them. But nobody knows for sure.

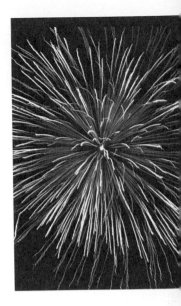

How did fireworks come to be? Again, we can only guess. But chances are, they began with an accident!

The colors in fireworks come from chemicals. The exploding chemicals make fireworks as noisy as they are. Maybe, long ago, chemicals cooking in a pot bubbled over into the cooking fire. They hit other chemicals in the fire and exploded. Blam! Can you imagine what a surprise that must have been?

For many, many years people everywhere have celebrated special days with the wonderful sights and sounds of fireworks. Over the years people have learned to use fireworks to put on more and more amazing shows. They made many different kinds of fireworks. Some of these are rockets, firecrackers, fire fountains, and pinwheels.

Now there are even fireworks that make fantastic pictures in the air. They make pictures of people, of buildings, of waterfalls, even of waving flags! These fireworks are called "set pieces."

Set pieces are made so that each glowing spark, after it bursts into the sky, floats slowly down. Then the sparks burn brightly at just the right spot on a specially treated metal frame.

Each metal frame is in the shape of a picture. Because the dark frames on the ground cannot be seen before the sparks explode, the set pieces have a very special beauty.

Slowly, the bright sparks disappear into the night. Look! The last red, white, and blue dots of color in the flag are still glowing.

Fireworks bring us fun and beauty. But it is important to remember that they can also be dangerous. When fireworks get into the wrong hands, they can cause very bad accidents. Yet, in the right hands, fireworks can save lives! Do you know how?

Imagine that a ship is lost on the high seas or that a car has broken down on a busy road. What do you think someone could use to call for help? Bright flares!

Flares are shot off! People see their color and light. Soon, help is on the way.

Fireworks are bright, noisy—and sometimes, lifesaving—magic!

Miss Tibbett's Typewriter

Eve Merriam

Part One
One Key Among Many

Miss Tibbett lived in the city. She lived in a small room with a big sweet-potato plant, a striped cat, and an old typewriter.

She liked the sweet-potato plant even though it grew so much that it wound all around the room and covered the front door. She liked the cat even though it scratched up her tables and chairs. And she liked the typewriter even though it wasn't in the best working order.

Miss Tibbett liked the clackety sound the keys made when her fingers pressed down on them. She also liked the sound of the little bell when she came to the end of a line: *ping*. And another line: *ping*. Line after line, all the way down the page: *ping, ping, ping, ping*.

There were many keys to press. There were keys with numbers and keys with all kinds of marks. There were marks that sounded slow and lazy and marks that sounded excited.

Then there were the rows of keys with letters. The top row went QWERTYUIOP. Miss Tibbett thought it sounded like a morning bird calling her to get up. QWERTYUIOP, QWERTYUIOP! Even if she tried to hide under the covers, the QWERTYUIOP bird would keep on calling: qwertyuiop, qwertyUIOP!

The next row of letters went ASDFGHJKL. ASDFGHJKL? Miss Tibbett knew what that meant. ASDFGHJKL was the sound of an elephant's sneeze. ASDFGHJKL! Kachoo, kachoo. Bless you, elephant.

The last row of letters went ZXCVBNM. Now here Miss Tibbett was not so sure. Some days it seemed to her that ZXCVBNM was the name of an animal that lived millions of years ago.

Yet, on other days, it seemed more likely that the ZXCVBNM was a creature from another planet. Was the creature a friendly one? She wasn't at all sure.

Taken all together, the three rows of QWERT-YUIOP and ASDFGHJKL and ZXCVBNM made up the whole alphabet. If she were to use each and every letter, Miss Tibbett could type out: *The quick brown fox jumps over the lazy dog.* That would use all twenty-six letters.

But there was one key that always got stuck. Miss Tibbett didn't let it bother her, though. She kept right on typing, listening to the little bell go *ping* at the end of every line. After all, what if one key didn't work. What was just one when there were so many?

Miss Tibbett lived around the corner from a car repair shop. One morning, the owner, Mr. Golden, was on his way to work. He heard the sounds of clackety-clack-clack *ping* coming from Miss Tibbett's room. Mr. Golden asked her if she would type a sign for him to put in the window of his shop.

Miss Tibbett nodded and smiled. She was pleased that her old typewriter could be so useful. She would make a sign for Mr. Golden's shop. And then she would make signs for some of the other shops, too. How busy and happy she would be!

Next day, she went to the car repair shop, all ready with her sign for the window. Mr. Golden was putting a new tire on a car and his helper was fixing a bumper that had been bent. Miss Tibbett let them work. She hung the sign in the window herself and then walked away, smiling. How good it felt to be useful! But Mr. Golden scratched his head when he looked at the sign. It said:

```
Come to Golden's Car Repair Shop.
  We  ix  lats and  enders.
```

Miss Tibbett had gone on to type up a card for Mr. Bremen, the tailor. His sign read:

```
Let us  it you with  ine  urs.
  Our prices are  air.
```

Then Miss Tibbett left the sign she made for Mrs. Able at the airline office. It said:

```
Dreaming about  araway places?
Why not go on a  un- illed trip
to  rance?  You can  ly now and
pay later.
```

And last she left this card for Mr. and Mrs. Howard at the drug store. It read:

```
eeling not so good?  Call on us to
ill your every pill need.  We  ill
orders  ast.
```

After leaving all her signs, she walked quickly home to type a letter to her sister, who lived in another state. The words came out this way on Miss Tibbett's old typewriter:

```
Dear Isabel,
It must be nice and warm now on your
 arm.  Here there is  rost under  oot.
Some days I think I am going to  reeze.
I have to wear  ur gloves.  With love.
```

"Oh, dear," Miss Tibbett said to her cat, "I think I better not type any more today." Miss Tibbett took the letter for her sister to the mailbox on the corner.

All the storekeepers ran up to her, holding the cards she had typed for them. "We can't use these! Just look!"

Part Two

A Typewriter with a Mind of Its Own

Miss Tibbett took her typewriter to the repair shop. "Please do something," she said. "Everything I type seems to need that stuck key."

"All right," said the repair man. "But it's a very old machine. I can't promise that something else won't go wrong."

"Please do what you can," said Miss Tibbett. "I want so much to have a floor and friends and flowers. I want to be able to kick a football or float in the lake or fly a kite."

The typewriter came back from the repair shop. Miss Tibbett opened the case and put a piece of paper in the machine. She began to type.

```
I feel fantastic and fine.
I can fly.  I can make a fire.
I can make a fence or a fort.
I can grow fat or flat.
I can even find a friend.
Finally, I'm free!
```

How fresh, how fine, how free-flowing all those new-found F's looked. Now she could even type up a menu for the restaurant, and not have to worry about Friday's fish dinner.

And here is how it came out on her fixed-up typewriter:

```
Special Seafood Dinner


             Fish soup
 roiled shrimp with  oiled egg sauce
        oston  aked  eans
           rown  read
        oston cream pie
```

By now, Miss Tibbett had learned to look over what she typed. So, as soon as she saw the way the menu came out, she ran to the typewriter repair shop again. The repair man was out on a call, so she typed a note for him and left the machine. Her note said:

```
As you will see, the key you
fixed is now fine,  ut another key is
either  ent or  roken. I need it  adly,
and  eg you to take care of it.  I will
  e  ack as soon as I go to the  ank and
then  uy a  ook, a new  icycle  ell,
and a  ig  unch of  alloons for  illy's
 irthday party.  He is my  rother's son.
```

When she returned, the typewriter was ready. The repair man told her, "I hope everything will be all right this time. I fixed the broken B key. You can test it for yourself and see how it works now."

Miss Tibbett pressed down on it. "Better," she said. "Now I can begin again. Good-by," and she went home.

How glad she was that she didn't have to worry any more about the broken B key. Now whatever she typed could be beautiful.

She typed out a card for little Billy's birthday present. It said:

```
Dear Billy,
   ow muc  I  ope you  ave a very
   appy birt day.
```

Miss Tibbett looked over what she had typed and shouted, "Elp!"

Back she went to the typewriter repair shop. "Please," she said, "please, please, please fix it again for me. I really cannot get along without a hand or a home or a heart! I need that H key, and I also need all the others. Please try to keep them all in line."

"I'll do the best I can," said the typewriter man. "Leave the machine here for a few days and I'll look it all over."

Miss Tibbett came for her typewriter later in the week. The repair man had a big smile on his face. "All fixed for you. I tested the whole alphabet. Now the quick brown fox jumps over the lazy dog with no trouble. You can use every letter from now on."

"How wonderful," Miss Tibbett smiled. "Now I'll be able to have apples and baseballs and cats and doorbells and eggs and forks and gloves and hats and ice cream and jump ropes and kittens and laps and mornings and noises and oceans and pianos and questions and rain and sunlight and trees and uncles and valleys and windows and X rays and yo-yos and even a zoo!"

"All of them," the typewriter man nodded. "All twenty-six letters are now in order."

"Oh, thank you," said Miss Tibbett, and she paid him for his work.

"Here," said the repair man. "I'll use your machine to show that you paid me."

He handed a note to her and it said:

Lend Me an Ear

Sometimes words don't really mean what they say. They say one thing, but they mean something else. Read this sentence:

Will you lend me your ear?

This sentence does not mean that you should take off your ear and give it to me. It means: "Will you listen to me?"

Now read each numbered sentence below. Then choose an answer that tells what the sentence *really* means. Write the answer on your paper.

1. Keep your eye on the ball.
    a. Take out your eye and put it on the ball.
    b. Watch the ball very carefully.

2. Sandy was tickled pink when she won.
   a. Someone tickled Sandy until she was pink.
   b. Sandy was happy when she won.

3. Ben's cold gave him a frog in his throat.
   a. Ben had to keep clearing his throat.
   b. A cold put a frog in Ben's throat.

4. This dinner is fit for a king and queen.
   a. Only a king and queen will eat this dinner.
   b. This is a very good and very special dinner.

5. We'll all be in the same boat if it snows today.
   a. We'll all go on a boat trip down the river in the snow.
   b. We'll all have the same problem if it snows today.

6. He laughed his head off at that joke.
   a. He thought the joke was very funny.
   b. He laughed so hard that his head fell off.

The Bravest Babysitter

Barbara Greenberg

Part One
The Thunderstorm

The doorbell rang, and Lisa galloped
over to help Mother open the door.
Heather, Lisa's favorite babysitter, walked
in. Heather bent down and said, "Hi, Lis.
You got a haircut. Now I can tickle you
right here on the back of your neck."

"What do you have on?" asked Lisa. She
opened Heather's coat. Heather had come
right from hockey practice. Under her long
coat she wore short shorts. Purple and
orange stripes chased each other around
her knee socks.

Lisa always had a good time with Heather. Heather liked to read books aloud, and she laughed hard at the silly parts and made her voice spooky for the scary parts. She was good at drawing, and she called Lisa "Lis."

Mother left, and Lisa and Heather got to work on a collage. Lisa liked to paste bumpy and smooth and bright-colored things all together on paper to make a design. This time she got big macaroni and small macaroni and some white buttons and brown buttons and a big shiny gold one. Heather cut out pictures from a magazine.

It started raining while they were working on the collage. It was a rough windy rain. It beat against the house and rattled the windows.

Suddenly the darkness outside got white with light, and then thunder rumbled through the sky.

"Oh, no. Thunder!" said Heather. She dropped the scissors and held onto the arms of the chair.

"Get ready. Here comes another one," she said after the next flash of lightning.

"What's the matter, Heather?" asked Lisa. "Are you scared?"

229

"Scared? Who's scared of a little thunder," said Heather when it was quiet again. "Now, listen, you thunder, you'll have to whisper please," yelled Heather.

Lisa laughed.

"Oh, no. Here comes more," said Heather. And she put her hands over her ears and squeezed her eyes shut.

"My mother always tells me to keep busy so I don't think so much about the thunder," Lisa said. "So, let's paste."

Lisa pasted her big macaroni and small macaroni and her white buttons and brown buttons and her big shiny gold button on some paper. She loved sticking her fingers in the paste and making collages, and she didn't think about the thunder.

But Heather wasn't paying attention to what she was doing. She pasted a picture right onto the table instead of onto the paper.

"Oh, no," said Lisa. "Look what you did. Let's think of something else to do. Do you want to read me a story?"

Lisa and Heather snuggled together in the soft armchair in the living room. Heather read a story.

Part Two
Who Is Brave?

There was a blaze of lightning and a bang of thunder. Heather sank lower into the chair and pulled Lisa down with her. Heather went on reading, but she didn't laugh now at the silly parts or make her voice spooky for the scary parts. She read and then looked out of the window and then read again and looked out of the window again. She kept losing her place.

"Let's play dress-up instead," said Lisa at last, and she dragged out her box full of old clothes. She draped a shawl around her shoulders, and she put a floppy hat, piled high with cherries and feathers, on her head. She pulled out a long dress and gave it to Heather.

But Heather got all tangled up in the dress. First she put one arm where the head should go. Then she put her head where the arm should go. Finally she put it on right.

Then Lisa pulled out a pair of shoes and gave them to Heather. But Heather put the shoes on the wrong feet.

There was another flash of light. Then *rumble, roar, crash* went the thunder.

"That was a loud one," said Heather.

"It will stop soon," said Lisa.

"You're brave, Lis," said Heather.

"Let's draw with crayons," said Lisa.

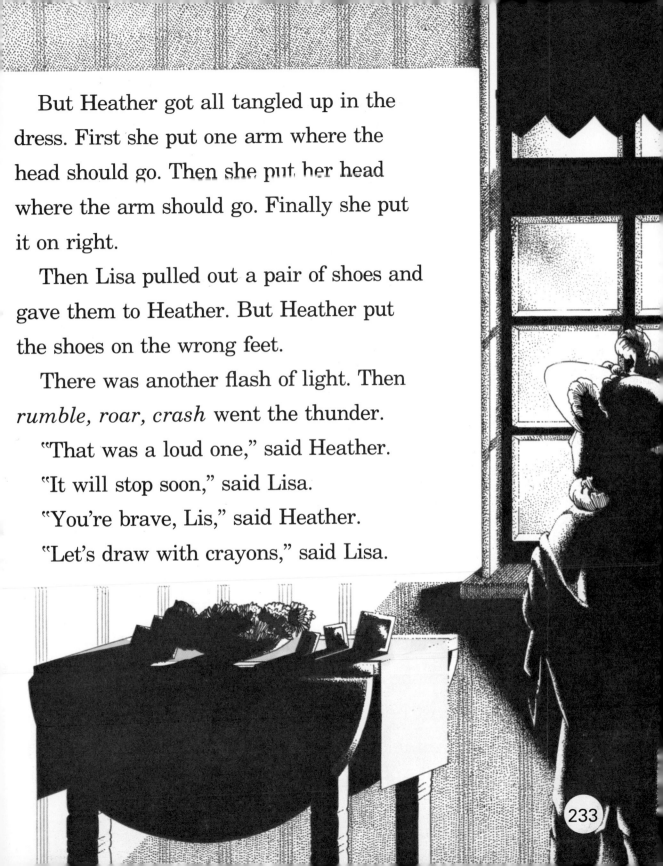

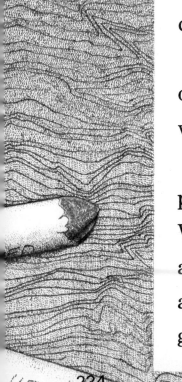

Lisa drew a picture of a sunny day with red and yellow flowers and green stems and a big, round, orange sun. Heather drew a picture of a rainstorm with a streak of lightning across the sky.

"I like yours better," said Heather.

"Here. It's for you," said Lisa.

It was Lisa's bedtime. She put on her pajamas and got ready for bed. But Heather said, "You may stay up tonight until the rain stops. Let's keep each other company a little while longer."

"Sometimes when there's thunder outside, my mother puts on a record and we dance," Lisa said.

Lisa and Heather chose a record and played it loud. Heather loved to dance. When she danced, her long hair flapped against her back. Lisa hopped and jumped and tumbled on the floor, but she couldn't get her short hair to flap like Heather's.

When the record was over, Heather said, "Look, it's stopped raining. There's no more thunder. You'd better go to sleep now. Would you like me to tuck you in?"

"No," said Lisa. "I'll tuck myself in tonight."

"You're a very good babysitter, Lis," said Heather.

"I know," said Lisa. "I hope there's thunder the next time you come so I can take care of you again. I like being a babysitter."

QUIET MAGIC

Judith Adams

You are at the circus. You can hear the brass band. You can smell the candy and the peanuts. Look! There, in the big ring, the lion tamer is waiting for the big cats to come out.

Slowly the big cats come, growling. They don't look friendly. But the lion tamer is not afraid. In one hand he holds a hoop; in the other, a whip. One by one, the lions jump through the hoop. They run into the open cage as the lion tamer follows them with his eyes.

But wait! One lion won't jump! The lion tamer holds the hoop over his head. His mouth opens in a wide smile. Then he slowly brings the hoop down. He circles the ring, never once taking his eyes off the lion.

What if the lion jumps for the tamer's throat? You sit and wait, afraid to breathe. Oh, there goes the lion! It jumps through the hoop and runs into the cage. The lion tamer is safe! He smiles and bows. Everyone claps!

Now look again at the lion tamer. He is not in a circus ring after all. He is standing alone on an empty stage. The circus ring, the cage, and the lions are make-believe.

The man's name is Marcel Marceau. Look at his face. It is covered with white makeup. In the picture on the left-hand page, he is wearing white pants, a gray vest over a striped T-shirt, and a hat with a flower in it.

When Marceau wears this outfit, he is Bip the Clown. Bip plays many roles. He may be a lion tamer, an ice skater, a firefighter, even a butterfly catcher.

Marcel Marceau is a mime. His art is called pantomime. Mimes use their faces and their bodies to show us an imaginary world. Good mimes make this imaginary world seem like a real world.

Marceau pantomimes a person trying to walk against the wind — you can almost feel the wind. When he pantomimes a person in a cage, you can almost see the bars of the cage. You know just how the locked-up person feels.

Marcel Marceau makes pantomime seem easy. But he practices very hard so he can "speak" with his body. He watches people of every age, size, and shape as they move. He practices doing many things with his body. He sits, leans, digs, climbs, carries, pulls. He practices these things over and over again. He wants us to "see" everything.

At last he is sure that he can make us see the chair he sits on, the wall he leans on, the soil he digs. We can also see the stairs he climbs, the plate he carries, and the rope he pulls. He can make us see things that aren't there at all!

Finally, in his act, Marcel Marceau puts all the pieces together. He then brings us the magic of stories without words. He is a person at a party, a park full of people, or a brave lion tamer facing a ring of lions.

The Jar of Tassai

Grace Moon

Part One

Tassai's Secret

Tassai lived on the top of a mesa that looked far out over the Painted Desert. The air was as clear as thin ice. It even made the faraway mountains and blue hills look nearer than they really were. Tassai was a Pueblo Indian girl. She was as brown as a nut that has dried in the sun. She liked to lie on the edge of the mesa. She would look over the desert and dream long dreams.

But Tassai did not often have time for dreams. There was too much work for her to do. Tassai worked with her mother in the little fields at the foot of the mesa. It was not hard work, and it had magic in it. It had the magic of watching green things spring up out of the ground where only brown earth had been before.

Tassai brought water, too, from the spring at the foot of the mesa. She carried it up the steep trail in jars. For hours each day she ground the red and blue and yellow grains of corn. She cooked when her mother needed her help. She also knew where to find the grass that her mother wove into baskets.

There was one thing Tassai did that no one knew about. This was because she did it only at times when no eyes were watching. She was making a jar from clay that she had found in a secret place. There the earth was smooth as honey to the touch and dark in color. Not even her mother knew that Tassai was working at this jar. It was Tassai's secret.

She shaped it and smoothed it. She knew how to do this from watching her mother. The most beautiful jar of all started to form itself in her hands. She painted fine black lines on it and baked it a golden brown. Tassai thought that there had never been a jar as lovely as this one. She carefully wrapped it in a blanket and put it away in a safe place.

All through the hours while she
worked in the fields, Tassai thought
of her jar. In her thoughts a little
song sang itself over and over again
until her feet danced to the music
of it:

It is so beautiful,
My big, round jar!
So round and beautiful!
Only the Moon,
When it walks on the edge of the world
Is like my jar.
Round and smooth it is,
And has a shine that sings!
Maybe the Moon has come to me
To be my jar!

Not long before Tassai made
her jar, the Governor of the Pueblo
called the people of the town together.
They gathered in the little open place
where meetings were held. He told
them that the people of three towns
were going to meet for a time of
dancing and feasting. He asked that
each man, woman, and child bring
to the feast something he or she had
made. Prizes would be given for the
very best things brought to the feast.

Everyone was very excited about
the Governor's news. There was much
talking and planning of what should
be done. Tassai was excited from the
first. She could hardly wait for the
time to come.

Part Two
The Big Day

The day itself was wonderful. There
was a feel in the air that was different. Tassai felt that she could not
walk or talk or even breathe as she
did on other days. The open place
in the town was bright with color.
It was like a fair.

There were good smells and different sounds everywhere. There were
baskets and pottery and woven things
all spread out for everyone to see.
There were silver bracelets and rings
and belts. There were bright blankets
and things of leather and wood. There
were ears of corn that were bigger
than any Tassai had ever seen before.
There were beaded shoes and nets
for carrying things. There were little
cakes made of pine nuts and seeds.
There was good food cooking in pots.

248

Tassai was one of the very last to come into the open place on that big day. She had been busy since sunup, helping her mother. At last she was free. She picked up the blanket in which her jar was wrapped and ran to the open place. There she stood, holding the blanket close to her side.

The Governor of the Pueblo moved from place to place with some elderly people. They looked long and closely at each of the many things that had been brought. With them was a visitor from a nearby town. He had come with his little daughter to see the dancing and feasting.

The little girl danced ahead of them as they walked. She looked at everything with bright eyes.

When the people had seen everything else, they started walking up to Tassai. She was nervous now. Maybe they would not think her jar was beautiful. Others began to gather around. They had not known that Tassai would have anything to show.

"Maybe it is not very good," she said in a voice that was so low no one heard her. "Maybe it—" Then her words would not come at all.

When she opened the blanket, the beautiful jar was not there. She had not noticed that there were two piles of blankets in the room of her home. The one she had picked up in her hurry held only an old corncob doll.

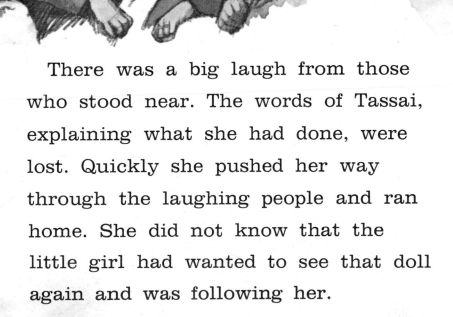

There was a big laugh from those who stood near. The words of Tassai, explaining what she had done, were lost. Quickly she pushed her way through the laughing people and ran home. She did not know that the little girl had wanted to see that doll again and was following her.

The house of Tassai was the last one in the little town. It was on the very edge of the mesa top. She ran into the door. She did not notice that the little girl who had followed her had stopped suddenly just outside the doorway. The child was watching, with wide eyes full of fear, a snake that picked up its head from behind a big stone. It was a rattlesnake. It moved its flat head closer and closer to the little girl. She gave one loud cry as Tassai came out of the door with the jar in her arms. Tassai had thrown off the blanket and held just the jar in her arms.

There was no time to think. There was no time to call for help. Tassai did the only thing she could do. With all her might she threw the jar at the rattlesnake. It broke into many pieces on the rock, and the snake lay flat and still.

The little girl did not make another sound. Her father, who had heard her first cry, came running. He held her in his arms.

For the first second, Tassai thought only that the rattlesnake was dead. Then she thought of her jar. No one would call it beautiful now. She picked up a little broken piece. As she was looking at it, the father of the little girl took it from her hand.

"That was a beautiful jar," he said slowly. "Did you make it?"

Tassai nodded her head. The man looked at the broken jar again, and said, "I cannot thank you enough for what you have done for my daughter. Your beautiful jar would certainly have won a prize. If only I could think of a way to make up for the lost prize——"

At this point, the Governor, who had been looking on, spoke. "Prizes were to be given for the most beautiful things brought to this feast. Now I would like to give a prize to Tassai who has shown us that a deed can be very beautiful, too." With this he handed her a prize. The elderly people nodded their heads with pride. The children who were gathered around clapped and cheered.

The little girl whom Tassai saved came up and smiled at Tassai. She asked, "Can I see your pretty corncob doll again?" Tassai held out her hand to the little girl and soon they were walking together toward Tassai's house. Now Tassai felt very happy. It did not matter that her jar was broken. She could make another, even more beautiful.

What Happened Here?

A *paragraph* is a group of sentences. The sentences all tell about one thing. The *main-idea sentence* tells the most important idea. The *detail sentences* tell about the main idea.

ACTIVITY A   Read the paragraph below. Then read the numbered questions. Choose an answer and write it on your paper.

There are many kinds of imaginary monsters. Some monsters, like Mermaids, are part human and part animal. Others, like Dragons, are scary. Unicorns are not so scary.

1. What is the main-idea sentence?
   a. Unicorns are not so scary.
   b. There are many kinds of imaginary monsters.

2. Which detail sentence tells about scary monsters?
   a. Others, like Dragons, are scary.
   b. Unicorns are not so scary.

ACTIVITY B   Read the paragraph. Then write the answer to each question on your paper

You can learn many things about animals at the zoo. You can see animals from all over the world. You can learn how each animal looks. You can also learn how it acts and what it eats.

1. What is the main-idea sentence?
2. Which detail sentence tells what you can see at the zoo?
   a. You can learn how each animal acts and what it eats.
   b. You can see animals from all over the world.

ACTIVITY C   Write this main-idea sentence.
    Popcorn is an unusual food.
Now choose detail sentences that go with the main-idea sentence. Write them on your paper.
1. It is kept in a cage at the zoo.
2. It needs to be dry to pop.
3. When cooked, you can write with it.
4. When cooked, each piece explodes.

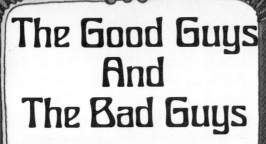

The Good Guys And The Bad Guys

OSMOND MOLARSKY

Part One
The Roller Skates

"Out!" said Parker's mother. "Out! Out! Out!"
For five days, Parker had been inside
watching television while he had a bad cold.
"Outside now and get some fresh air!"

Outside the sudden sunlight made Parker close his eyes. When he opened them, his friend Doug was just a blur.

"What's been happening?" said Parker, as if he'd been away for weeks. "Any action?"

"Lot of it," said Doug. "Ten kids got their roller skates stolen."

"Ten kids got their skates stolen? What kids?"

"All the ones that left their skates out in their yards or on the sidewalk."

"Rustlers!" Parker whispered. "We've got to round them up—get some action."

"Did they get your skates?" Doug asked.

"No," said Parker.

"Mine neither," said Doug. "So I guess it's none of our business."

"We've got to catch them," Parker said. "They're a threat to the whole valley."

Doug wondered what valley Parker was talking about. "How are we going to round them up?" he asked.

"Easy," said Parker. "We get the evidence. Then, we tail them and bring them in."

Parker was blinking in the bright light. Doug could see he had been watching a lot of television. "How do we get the evidence?" he asked.

"Snoop around until we get some leads," Parker said.

"What do we do then? Tell the police?"

"Are you out of your head? Can you picture a lot of police officers marching around backyards and down in cellars looking for roller skates? The cons would move the evidence so fast it would take your breath away."

"I thought they were rustlers."

"Rustlers...cons...they're bad guys, that's what they are."

"Couldn't police officers in plain clothes catch them?"

"Get with it, friend. You can spot police officers every time, at sixty yards."

"How?" said Doug.

"By the bumps under their coats."

"What bumps?"

"Their guns, naturally. Don't you *ever* watch TV?" Parker asked.

"Sure," Doug said, but he didn't say how much. Mostly, he just read books.

"We've got to do this alone," Parker said.

"When do we start?" Doug asked. He was beginning to think that maybe a little action wouldn't be bad.

"We start right now," said Parker. "First, we split up. You go one way. I go another. Then we snoop around."

"Where do we snoop around?"

"Anywhere. Play it by ear. But don't let anyone guess what you're doing."

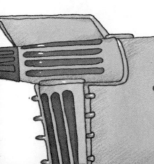

"How do we keep them from guessing?"

"Like you don't come right out and ask if anyone's seen a whole lot of roller skates in someone's cellar."

"What do you say?"

"You say something like: *I wish I knew where I could buy a pair of used roller skates for sixty cents.*"

"I've already got roller skates," said Doug.

"I know that! You don't really want to buy any. The idea is, if you say that, someone might say: *I know a kid who has some to sell.* Then you ask who, and that kid could be the crook who took all the skates so he could sell them. You know he didn't steal them all to use for himself. He'd have to have a hundred feet!"

Doug was amazed at how smart Parker had gotten from watching television. Maybe he should watch more television himself and get smarter.

"I'll go this way," said Parker. "You go that way. I'll call you tonight, and we'll see what we have."

That night at dinner, just as Doug was finishing his cake, he got a call.

"This is Bloodhound," a voice said, trying to sound deep.

"Is that you, Parker?"

"This is Bloodhound!" the voice said again, deeper than before. "Is this Barracuda?"

Doug could tell it was Parker, so he said, "Yes, Bloodhound, this is Barracuda."

"Did you find out anything?" Parker asked.

"Not much," said Doug. "I asked some kids if they knew where I could buy some used skates for sixty cents. One kid was on skates, and he kept falling down. He said he'd sell me his skates for twenty-five cents."

"Did he look strange?"

"He just looked like he couldn't skate," said Doug.

"Keep your eye on him," Parker said. "The falling down could be a cover. Crooks are very smart."

"Will do," Doug answered. That's the way he'd heard it on television. "You have any luck, Bloodhound?"

"Some kids said I could buy all the skates I wanted for sixty cents at the Good Will store."

"What do you make of that?"

"I'll watch 'em," said Parker. "Listen, Barracuda, keep your eyes open and call me after school tomorrow."

"Right," said Doug.

In the next few days, five more kids said their skates had been stolen. Mabel Drummond's mother called the police. They said they were too busy to look into missing roller skates.

"You see?" said Parker. "The case is in our hands."

Now they began to tail some shady types. Chester Matson, for one. Chester liked to swap, and he was so fast, he could swap you out of anything you had before you knew it. Once he swapped Parker out of a Boy Scout knife for a tin good-luck ring that never brought him any good luck. Parker said to Doug, "You can't believe that guy. Watch him. He may lead us to something." Parker himself tailed Chester for three days, but he never led them to any stolen skates.

They also tailed Pete Slocum. No one had anything on Pete. But sometimes he came up to you so quietly when you were talking to someone, you didn't even know he was listening.

"Tail him wherever he goes and tell me about it, Barracuda," Parker ordered. Doug tried, but every now and then he would lose sight of Pete. Then he would turn around, and there Pete would be, behind him.

"*You* tail him, Bloodhound," Doug told Parker after a few days. "He has me going around in circles."

"You're doing fine," said Parker. "Just don't let him get the drop on you."

The next day, on the way to school, Doug saw something he thought was very strange. It was Mr. Tyson B. Tyson walking along, looking very mad, carrying two pairs of roller skates. Mr. Tyson was the man who lived in the yellow house up on the hill. Sometimes he did funny things.

TYSON B. TYSON

Once a man threw a half-eaten peach onto the sidewalk. Mr. Tyson picked it up, caught up with the man and said, "You dropped something, sir." Then, pushing it—all sticky—in the pocket of the man's coat, he gave it a hard pat and went on his way.

"I saw him with two pairs of skates, not just one," Doug told Parker.

"That man would never take skates," Parker said. "He must have bought them for his grandchildren. Anyway, forget him. I've got just the trap to catch the crook. Listen to this. You leave your skates out where they can be stolen, on the sidewalk," he began.

"Stolen? What for?" asked Doug.

"They won't really be stolen," said Parker. "They're just bait. We tie a string on them. The string runs up to a window of your house. You tie the other end of the string to those bells your mom has hanging on a rope. When the crook tries to take the skates, the bells will ring. Then we'll run out and catch the crook with the skates."

"Good idea," Doug said. Parker looked very proud of himself. "Only let's use your skates," Doug said.

"If that's the way you feel, all right, I will," said Parker.

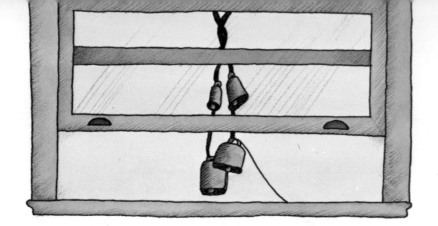

The next afternoon they set up the trap with Parker's skates for bait, and sat down to watch television. "This is going to be easy," Parker said. "Why didn't I think of it before?"

By five o'clock, they had been watching TV for two hours. "Don't you think we better take a look outside?" Doug asked.

"What for?" said Parker. "The bells will ring." On TV, a bear on skates was speeding down a hill, and Parker wanted to see what would happen when he got to the bottom.

Doug went outside anyway. In a second, he came back and said, "Your skates are gone, Bloodhound."

"They can't be gone," said Parker. "We'd have heard the bells ring when he picked them up."

"You're right," said Doug. "Only, he cut the string."

For just a second, Parker looked foolish. Then he looked grim. "A very smart crook," he said. "This means we're going to have to work even harder to catch him."

Part Two
The Posse

Friday afternoon, Parker called Doug and said, "We've got a break in the case, Barracuda."

"Spill it to me," said Doug. He had almost stopped reading books and was listening more closely now, on television, to the way a sleuth talks.

"You know Link Wilson, over on Weston Street?"

"Yes," said Doug. He was thinking of the great skate scooters Link made in his cellar and then sold.

"Well," Parker went on, "Link was pushing this neat skate scooter up Lincoln Street, and I said I thought it was neat. He told me he made it and did I want to buy one."

"What did you say?" asked Doug.

"I asked how much he wanted for it. A dollar, he said. So I said I'd take it, if I could pay him twenty-five cents a week. He said okay, but not that one. That was only a model. He said he was making a lot of them in his cellar, and maybe I'd like a blue one or a red one. So I said all right, let's go to his cellar, and we did."

"What did you see there?" asked Doug.

"I'm coming to that, Barracuda," Parker said. "I saw about five scooters. All different colors. Two of them had tags that said they were sold. Link said the boys had put some money down and were going to take them when they got the rest of the money."

"Which one did you pick?"

"A blue one with white shooting stars on it. I gave him twenty cents down. But get this— while he was putting a SOLD tag on it, I saw what we've been looking for."

"What was that, Bloodhound?"

"About twenty roller skates, plain as day, in the corner."

"Did you ask him where he got them?"

"No. I know where he got them."

"Did you see your roller skates there? The ones we used for bait?"

"I saw *three* pairs like mine."

"What do we do now?" Doug asked.

"I already did it. I called together a posse."

"A posse?" Doug never heard of a sleuth using a posse. But this was Parker's show.

"Who's in the posse?" asked Doug.

"All the kids who got their skates stolen," said Parker. "And that means Scrappy Bassett is in the posse, too."

SCRAPPY BASSETT

Doug knew Scrappy. Her real name was
Marlene, but her brothers called her Scrappy
because she could lick them. All five of them,
even though she was the smallest. She loved
to watch a small woman on television who
could floor crooks with one karate chop.
Scrappy knew all the moves and how to use
them. But her real secret was that she was
so small she made the other kids look mean
if they even tried to fight back.

Parker went on with his plan. "I'm going to get Link to the alley by Mr. Tyson B. Tyson's house. I told him I've got two kids who want to buy blue skate scooters with white stripes, and he's going to bring them. When he gets there, the posse will move into the gully from both ends, so he can't escape."

"I didn't know there was a gully around here," Doug said.

"The alley, dope!" Parker said. "Scrappy will work him over until he confesses."

"After Link confesses," Parker went on, "he'll lead us to the loot. If he made any of the skates into scooters, he'll have to give the whole scooter to the owner of the skates. That's justice."

"But what about all the other suspects?"

"What other suspects?"

"You know. Chester the Swapper. Pete, who's always around behind you. The kid who pretends to fall down all the time on his skates. Mr. Tyson B. Tyson..."

"Will you forget that man! Forget all the suspects! We've got this one cold. Just be at the gully at four o'clock tomorrow."

"I'll be there, Bloodhound," Doug answered and hung up.

The next day, everything came off just as Parker had planned. The posse split up and hid at the two ends of the alley beside Mr. Tyson's house. Link met Parker in the alley, he was pushing two beautiful skate scooters he had made.

"Where are the guys who want to buy the scooters?" Link asked Parker.

"They'll be here before you know it," said Parker, and with that, the posse jumped out and blocked the ends of the alley, seven at each end.

Link saw right away that he was trapped.

"What's the idea!" he said. He was really scared.

"What's the idea of taking roller skates!" Hamilton shouted, and the whole posse started to yell at Link from both ends of the alley. All but Scrappy Bassett. She didn't make a sound, just stood there looking mad.

"Let me handle this," Parker said. "Okay, what's the idea of taking roller skates? You better confess!"

"I didn't take any roller skates," Link said.

"Then where did you get the skates to make the scooters?"

"Where do you think? I buy them at the Good Will. Sixty cents a pair. I use the back and front of one skate to make a scooter. I find the wood and the boxes. My pop's a painter, and he gives me the paint left over from his jobs. I sell each scooter for one dollar, and I make seventy cents."

"Tell it to Scrappy Bassett," Parker said. "Go get him, Scrappy."

"Listen!" Link shouted. "A kid goes with me when I buy the skates to help me carry them home."

"Hold it, Scrappy," said Parker. "What kid?"

"Johnny Hawkins," said Link.

"Never heard of him," said Parker.

Doug went up to Parker and whispered in his ear. "I know Johnny Hawkins. He lives over on Green Street."

"Forget it. He's just trying to win time," Parker said. "Leave this to me. Let all rustlers learn something from this. Okay, Scrappy, let him have a karate chop."

Scrappy Bassett began to move in on Link. The posse closed in, too, to be close to the action and make sure Link didn't escape.

Doug felt sorry for Link, even if he was a bad guy. The way Scrappy was moving in on him didn't seem fair.

"Wait, everyone," Doug yelled suddenly. "Maybe it would be better to wait and find Johnny Hawkins and see if he would say he went to the Good Will with Link to buy the skates. In fact, the Good Will would remember if some kid came in there and bought a lot of skates. Someone could run down there and ask them. The posse could hold Link till the kid got back." When no one said anything, Doug said, "I'll go myself!"

While everyone watched, Doug broke away from the posse and rounded the corner on the run. He had just passed Mr. Tyson B. Tyson's house when something caught his eye. It slowed him down and turned him right around. "I never saw that before," Doug said to himself, walking back. "Mr. Tyson must have just put it up."

It was a white sign, taped to the brick wall in front of the house. At the top, it said, IMPORTANT NOTICE, hand-printed with crayon. But what had really caught Doug's eye as he raced past was a hand-drawn, crayon picture of roller skates.

Doug read the sign. Then he read it again, very slowly.

"Zowie!" he thought. "I better act fast!"

Tearing the sign down and holding onto it, he raced around the corner and back to the alley just in time. Scrappy had backed Link up against the wall of the posse. He couldn't escape now.

"Stop!" Doug shouted. "Stop! Link Wilson didn't do it!"

No one listened. Scrappy was winding up for a karate chop, just as the woman did it on television.

Doug acted fast. Still holding the sign, he crashed through the circle that had closed in to watch the action and caught Scrappy's arm, just as she was about to land one on Link. "Stop!" he shouted again, holding the sign high with his other hand. "Read this!"

Now Parker himself stepped in, took the sign from Doug, and read it. For about five seconds, he looked very foolish, but only for five seconds. Almost at once, he took over again. "All right, you coyotes!" he barked. "You, Scrappy! Lay off!"

"But I thought..."

"Never mind what you thought!" Then, turning to Link, he said, "Okay, Link. I guess you're clean. You're free to go."

What had happened? "Read the sign,"
Parker said, holding it up, so they could all
see it. One by one, they read it, then
they turned to Link. They gathered around
him, shook his hand, and pounded him on
the back.

"We thought you were a bad guy," Theodore Jenkins said.

"We were all wrong," said Peter Gidding.

"We're sorry," a lot of them said, all talking together.

"That's okay," said Link, as surprised as the others.

"Now, about those skate scooters," said Parker. "Here's some more money down for the blue one with the white shooting stars."

"I want one, too," said Johnny Crane.

Other kids were giving orders now. A green one with red stars. A blue one with gold stripes down the sides.

"Can you make me one with pictures of bluebirds on it?" That was Scrappy Bassett giving her order and pulling out twenty-five cents from her pocket.

Seven kids ordered skate scooters. It was a good business day for Link Wilson.

The others, led by Mabel Drummond, marched around to Mr. Tyson B. Tyson's yellow house, right next to the alley.

As for Doug, he went straight home. He had made up his mind to spend more time watching television. Then he would understand things a little better and always know, right from the start, if someone was one of the good guys or one of the bad guys. It gave him a bad feeling not to be sure.

In order to remember the day, he kept the sign that had saved Link Wilson from mob justice. He stuck it up in his room.

288

Sudden Storm

Lightning cuts a jagged path above me.
And thunder follows, ripping,
rolling, crashing.

The sunlight dims…

A sidewalk pool reflects
the black trees;

raindrops pepper
the pool's surface.

-Hilary Beckett

THE MEXICAN MUSEUM

Mexican art has found a new home in San Francisco, California. The Mexican Museum there shows only Mexican and Mexican-American art. It is the first Mexican museum outside of Mexico.

San Francisco is a perfect city for the museum. More than four million Mexican Americans live in California. They and many other Americans can visit the museum and enjoy the art of Mexico.

The director and founder of the museum is Mr. Peter Rodriguez. Mr. Rodriguez is an artist himself. When he was twenty-eight, he visited Mexico for the first time. There he saw the beautiful art of Mexico. He wanted others to see it, too.

Mr. Rodriguez worked on his dream of opening a museum for many years. Finally, on November 20, 1975, the Mexican Museum was opened. Mr. Rodriguez gave the museum his own collection of Mexican art. Since then, more than 2,500 pieces of art have been given to the museum. Much of the folk art was given by the Mexican people.

Today the museum shows collections of many different kinds of art. Visitors can learn about each collection from the museum staff. The staff gives talks, tours, and programs in both English and Spanish.

Lauro Lopez painted this still life. It is called "Bodegón Con Piña," which means "Still Life with a Pineapple." A still life is a group of things that do not move.

Jesus Reyes Ferreira began to paint when he was fifty-five years old. This little horse, "Caballito," was painted on thin paper.

Candelario Medrano Lopez
is a Mexican folk artist. He
made this colorful creature
known as a "Nagual." It
looks like a bull with a
human face.

Courtesy of the Mexican Museum

Courtesy of the Mexican Museum

Julia Lopez painted this
picture of a boy selling
flowers. In Spanish, the
painting is named "El
Vendedor de Flores."

Look Up the Words

A *glossary* is a kind of dictionary. There is a glossary at the back of this book. It has some of the important words you have read in this book. It tells you how to divide a word into its parts. It tells you how to say the word. It also tells you what the word means.

What if you needed to know about the word *pioneer*? Look up *pioneer* in the glossary. How is the word divided into its parts? What does it mean?

> **pi·o·neer** (pī′ə nēr′) a person who is the first to explore and settle a region.

ACTIVITY A   Look up each word below in the glossary. Write the parts of each word on your paper. Then write the meaning of each word.

1. at/ten/tion careful watching and listening

2. evidence   3. restaurant

4. magazine   5. celebrate

6. rhinoceros   7. imaginary

8. parsley   9. sleuth

ACTIVITY B   Now you know about these words.
Use each one to finish a sentence below.
Write the whole sentence on your paper.

1. Leroy likes to draw ___ monsters.
   ANSWER: Leroy likes to draw imaginary
   monsters.

2. An elephant is in a cage next to a ___.

3. Sandy ate dinner at a Hawaiian ___ .

4. We grow ___ in our garden.

5. The teacher asked everyone to pay ___
   to the person talking.

6. Alice read a ___ that was all about
   taking care of pets.

7. The ___ found out what happened to the
   silver bowls.

8. The paw marks were ___ that the cat
   had been there.

9. Everyone came to the beach to ___
   my birthday.

GOOD NEWS

An important part of learning is looking and listening. What you see and what you hear work together to help you understand what is happening around you.

Thinking About "Good News"

1. In "A Special Kind of Help," where does the main part of the action take place?
2. How could Lisa tell that Heather was unhappy about the thunderstorm?
3. Why did Tassai have to break her jar?
4. How did Doug save Link Wilson from the posse?
5. Why is the Mexican Museum found in San Francisco, California?
6. What are some important things you have learned by looking and listening?

Glossary

This glossary will help you to pronounce and to understand the meanings of some of the unusual or difficult words in this book.

The pronunciation of each word is printed beside the word in this way: **o·pen** (ō′pən). The letters, signs, and key words in the list below will help you read the pronunciation respelling. When an entry word has more than one syllable, a dark accent mark (′) is placed after the syllable that has the heaviest stress. In some words, a light accent mark (′) is placed after the syllable that receives a less heavy stress.

The pronunciation key, syllable breaks, accent mark placements, and phonetic respellings in this glossary are adapted from the Macmillan *Beginning Dictionary* (1981) and the Macmillan *School Dictionary* (1981). Other dictionaries may use other pronunciation symbols.

Pronunciation Key

a	bad	**i**	it	**o͞o**	food	**yo͞o**	music	ə	*stands for*
ā	cake	**ī**	ice	**oi**	oil	**v**	very		a *as in* ago
ä	father	**j**	joke	**ou**	out	**w**	wet		e *as in* taken
b	bat	**k**	kit	**p**	pail	**y**	yes		i *as in* pencil
ch	chin	**l**	lid	**r**	ride	**z**	zoo		o *as in* lemon
d	dog	**m**	man	**s**	sit	**zh**	treasure		u *as in* helpful
e	pet	**n**	not	**sh**	ship				
ē	me	**ng**	sing	**t**	tall				
f	five	**o**	hot	**th**	thin				
g	game	**ō**	open	**th**	that				
h	hit	**ô**	off	**u**	cup				
hw	white	**oo**	wood	**ur**	turn				

A

ac · ci · dent (ak′sə dənt) *n.*   something that happens for no apparent reason and is not expected.

ac · tion (ak′shən) *n.*   something that is done; an act.

ac · tive (ak′tiv) *adj.*   **1.** moving around much of the time. **2.** working.

ad · di · tion (ə dish′ən) *n.*   **1.** the adding of two or more numbers or things. **2.** the act of adding. **in addition to.** as well as; also.

ad · ven · ture (ad ven′chər) *n.*   **1.** something a person does that involves danger and difficulties. **2.** an exciting experience.

a · lo · ha (ə lō′ə) *n.*   a Hawaiian word that means "love."

al · pha · bet (al′fə bet′) *n.*   the letters or symbols that are used to write a language, arranged in their proper order.

an · ten · na (an ten′ə) *n.*   a metal rod or wire used to send out or receive radio or television signals.

ap · pear (ə pēr′) *v.*   to come into sight; to be seen.

ar · chi · tect (är′kə tekt′) *n.*   a person whose work is to design and draw plans for buildings.

ar · rive (ə rīv′) *v.*   **ar · rived,** **ar · riv · ing.**   to come to a place.

as · tro · naut (as′trə nôt′) *n.*   a person who flies in a spacecraft.

at · ten · tion (ə ten′shən) *n.*   careful watching or listening.

B

Bach (bok)   a German musician.

bar · ra · cu · da (bar′ə kōō′də) *n.*   a fierce fish that lives in warm seas.

barre (bär) *n.*   a handrail along the walls of a dance studio.

bat · tle (bat′əl) *n.*   a fight or struggle.

beard (bērd) *n.*   the hair that grows on a man's face.

beau · ty (byōō′tē) *n.*   a quality that makes a person or thing pleasing to look at or hear.

be · lov · ed (bi luv′id, bi luvd′) *adj.*   loved very much.

blan · ket (blang′kit) *n.*   a covering made of wool, nylon, or other material, used on beds to keep people warm.

bot · tle (bot′əl) *n.*   a container to hold liquids, usually made of glass or plastic. A bottle has a narrow neck that can be closed with a cap or stopper.

brace · let (brās'lit) *n.* a band or chain worn around the wrist as an ornament.

broad (brôd) *adj.* large from one side to the other; wide.

burn (burn) *v.* **burn · ed** or **burnt, burn · ing.** to set on fire; be on fire.

busi · ness (biz'nis) *n.* **1.** the work that a person does to earn a living. **2.** matter or affair.

butch · er (booch'ər) *n.* a person who cuts up and sells meat.

c

cel · e · brate (sel'ə brāt') *v.* **cel · e · brat · ed, cel · e · brat · ing.** to observe or honor a special day or event with ceremonies.

cel · lar (sel'ər) *n.* a room or group of rooms built underground.

cel · lo (chel'ō) *n.* a musical instrument that is like a violin.

cer · tain (sur'tən) *adj.* **1.** sure; positive. **2.** some; particular; known but not named.

chem · i · cal (kem'i kəl) *n.* a substance made by or used in chemistry.

cher · ry (cher'ē) *n. pl.,* **cher · ries.** a small, round red fruit with a smooth skin.

chic · o · ry (chik'ər ē) *n.* **1.** a plant used in salads. **2.** the root of this plant, dried, roasted, and ground for mixing with coffee or for making a drink like coffee.

Christ · mas (kris'məs) *n.* the celebration each year of the birth of Jesus Christ. Christmas falls on December 25.

cir · cus (sur'kəs) *n.* a show with trained animals and acrobats, clowns, and other people who do special things. A circus is often held in a large tent.

cli · mate (klī'mit) *n.* the usual weather conditions of a place.

cof · fee (kô'fē) *n.* a dark brown drink made from the roasted seeds of the coffee tree.

a bad, ā cake, ä father; e pet, ē me; i it, ī ice; o hot, ō open, ô off; oo wood, oo food; oi oil, ou out; th thin, th that; u cup, ur turn, yoo music; zh treasure; ə ago, taken, pencil, lemon, helpful

col · lage (kə läzh′) *n.* a picture made by pasting paper, cloth, metal, and other things on a surface.

com · fort · a · ble (kum′fər tə bəl) *adj.* at ease; giving comfort.

com · pa · ny (kum′pə nē) *n.* **1.** a guest or guests. **2.** companionship.

con (kon) *n.* a slang term for *convict.* A convict is a person who is serving a prison term.

con · trol pan · el (kən trōl′ pan′əl) a board on which dials or other controls are mounted.

cor · al (kôr′əl) *n.* a hard stony material made up of the skeletons of tiny sea animals.

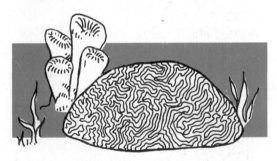

Co · rel · li (kə rel′ē) an Italian who wrote music.

cos · tume (kos′tōōm, kos′tyōōm) *n.* **1.** clothes worn in order to look like someone else. **2.** clothes worn at a particular time, in a particular place, or by particular people.

court (kôrt) *n.* an open space that is surrounded by walls.

cra · zy (krā′zē) *adj.* **1.** having a mind that is sick. **2.** foolish.

crea · ture (krē′chər) *n.* a living person or animal.

cur · tain (kur′tin) *n.* **1.** a piece of cloth hung across an open space. **2.** *theater.* the end of a scene or act indicated by the falling or closing of a curtain.

cus · tom (kus′təm) *n.* **1.** a way of acting that has become accepted by many people. **2.** the usual way that something is done; habit.

D

dan · ger · ous (dān′jər əs) *adj.* likely to cause something bad or harmful to happen.

de · li · cious (di lish′əs) *adj.* pleasing or delightful to the taste or smell.

de · sert (dez′ərt) *n.* a dry sandy area of land with few or no plants.

de · sign (di zīn′) *n.* an arrangement of different parts or colors; pattern.

dis · ap · pear (dis′ə pēr′) *v.* to go out of sight.

dis · cov · er (dis kuv′ər) *v.* to see or find out for the first time.

door · way (dôr′wā′) *n.*   an opening in a wall that leads in and out of a room or building.

drag (drag) *v.*   **dragged, drag · ging.**   to pull or move along slowly or heavily.

drug (drug) *n.*   a chemical or other substance that makes a change in a person's body. Most drugs are used to treat or cure diseases.

E

ear · ly (ur′lē) *adv.*   **1.** in or during the first part of a period of time. **2.** in the early part of the morning.

earn (urn) *v.*   to get as pay for work done.

E · gypt (ē′jipt) *n.*   a country in northeastern Africa.

eight (āt) *n.*   a number, one more than seven.—*adj.*   amounting to 8 in number.

eld · er · ly (el′dər lē) *adj.*   rather old.

en · ter · tain (en′tər tān′) *v.*   **1.** to keep interested and amused. **2.** to have as a guest.

es · cape (es kāp′) *v.*   **es · caped, es · cap · ing.**   to get away; get free.

es · pe · cial · ly (es pesh′ə lē) *adv.*   more than usually; particularly.

ev · i · dence (ev′ə dəns) *n.*   proof of something.

ex · cit · ed (ek sī′tid) *adj.*   stirred up; aroused.

ex · panse (eks pans′) *n.*   a wide, open area.

ex · pect (eks pekt′) *v.*   **1.** to look forward to. **2.** to think; suppose.

ex · per · i · ment (eks per′ə mənt) *n.*   a test that is used to discover or prove something.

ex · plain (eks plān′) *v.*   **1.** to make something plain or clear; tell the meaning of. **2.** to give or have a reason for.

ex · plode (eks plōd′) *v.*   **ex · plod · ed, ex · plod · ing.**   to burst suddenly and with a loud noise; blow up.

ex · plore (eks plôr′, eks plōr′) *v.*   **ex · plored, ex · plor · ing.**   to travel in unknown lands for the purpose of discovery.

a bad, ā cake, ä father; e pet, ē me; i it, ī ice; o hot, ō open, ô off; oo wood, ōo food; oi oil, ou out; th thin, th that; u cup, ur turn, yōo music; zh treasure; ə ago, taken, pencil, lemon, helpful

F

fan · tas · tic (fan tas'tik) *adj.* **1.** very strange; odd. **2.** very good; excellent.

fa · vor · ite (fā'vər it) *adj.* liked best.

fear (fēr) *n.* a strong feeling caused by knowing that danger, pain, or evil is near.

fif · ti · eth (fif'tē ith) *adj.* next after forty-ninth.

fla · vor (flā'vər) *n.* a particular taste.

float (flōt) *n.* a low, flat platform on wheels that carries an exhibit in a parade.—*v.* to rest on top of water or other liquids.

force (fôrs) *v.* **forced, forc · ing.** to make do something.

fort (fôrt) *n.* a strong building or area that can be defended.

fruit (frōot) *n.* the part of a plant that contains seeds. Oranges, apples, and nuts are fruits.

fur · nace (fur'nis) *n.* an enclosed place where heat is produced.

G

gal · lop (gal'əp) *v.* to run rapidly by leaps, as a horse.

gear (gēr) *n.* equipment for a particular purpose.

ger · bil (jur'bil) *n.* a small animal something like a mouse.

god (god) *n.* a being who is supposed to have special powers over the lives and doings of people. Legends are often about gods and goddesses.

gov · er · nor (guv'ər nər) *n.* a person who governs.

guess (ges) *v.* **1.** to form an opinion without having enough facts to be sure. **2.** to think; believe; suppose.

H

half (haf) *adv.* not completely; partly.

Han · del (hand'əl) a German musician.

harp · si · chord (härp'sə kôrd') *n.* a musical instrument with strings and a keyboard.

Ha · wai · i (hə wä'ē) *n.* a state of the United States.

heart (härt) *n.* **1.** the part of the body that pumps blood. **2.** the heart thought of as the center of a person's feelings.

hon · ey (hun'ē) *n.* a thick, sweet liquid made by bees.

hot · cake (hot'cāk') *n.* a pancake.

hus · band (hus'bənd) *n.* a man who is married.

I

i · mag · i · nar · y (i maj'ə när'ē) *adj.* existing only in the mind; not real.

in · de · pend · ence (in'di pen' dəns) *n.* freedom from the control of another or others.

in · stru · ment (in'strə mənt) *n.* **1.** a device used for doing a certain kind of work; tool. **2.** a device for producing musical sounds.

is · land (ī'lənd) *n.* a body of land that is completely surrounded by water. An island is smaller than a continent.

J

Ju · ly (joo lī') *n.* the seventh month of the year.

jus · tice (jus'tis) *n.* the quality of being fair and right.

K

ka · ra · te (kə ra'tē) *n.* a Japanese system of unarmed self-defense.

key · board (kē'bôrd') *n.* a set or row of keys. A piano has a keyboard.

king · dom (king'dəm) *n.* a country that is ruled by a king or queen.

L

lac · quer (lak'ər) *n.* a material something like paint or varnish.

a bad, ā cake, ä father; e pet, ē me; i it, ī ice; o hot, ō open, ô off; oo wood, o͞o food; oi oil, ou out; th thin, th that; u cup, ur turn, yo͞o music; zh treasure; ə ago, taken, pencil, lemon, helpful

la · dy (lā′dē) *n. pl.,* **la · dies. 1.** any woman. **2.** a woman of high social position. **3.** a girl or woman who is polite or who has good manners.

lan · guage (lang′gwij) *n.* human speech; spoken or written words.

laun · dry (lôn′drē) *n.* sheets, clothes, and other things that have been washed or are to be washed.

lau · rel (lôr′əl) *n.* an evergreen tree that has stiff, pointed leaves.

law · yer (lô′yər) *n.* a person who knows a great deal about law.

leg · end (lej′ənd) *n.* a story passed down through the years that many people have believed but that is not entirely true.

lev · el (lev′əl) *adj.* **1.** having a flat surface; even. **2.** at the same height.

lose (lōōz) *v.* **lost, los · ing. 1.** to have no longer; be without. **2.** to fail to keep.

M

ma'am (mam) *n.* a contraction for *madam. Madam* is a word used as a polite form of address to a woman.

mac · a · ro · ni (mak′ə rō′nē) *n.* a food made from flour paste or dough.

ma · chine (mə shēn′) *n.* a device made up of a number of moving or fixed parts that work together to do some particular job. A lawn mower, a typewriter, and a printing press are machines.

mag · a · zine (mag′ə zēn′, mag′ə zēn′) *n.* a printed collection of stories, articles, and pictures, usually bound in a paper cover.

man · age (man′ij) *v.* **man · aged, man · ag · ing.** to control or direct; be able to.

Mar · ceau, Mar · cel (mär sō′, mär səl′)

may · or (mā′ər) *n.* the person who is the official head of a city.

med · i · cine (med′ə sin) *n.* a drug or other substance used to prevent or treat disease or to relieve pain.

men · u (men′yōō′) *n.* a list of food that is available in a restaurant or other eating place.

mer · chant (mur′chənt) *n.* **1.** a person whose business is buying and selling things. **2.** a person who owns or runs a store.

me · sa (mā′sə) *n.* a flat-topped hill or mountain with steep sides.

met · al (met′əl) *n.* a substance that has a shiny surface, can be molted, and can conduct heat and electricity. Iron, copper, and brass are metals.

Milk · y Way (mil′kē wā′) a cloudy white area that can be seen across the sky at night. It is made up of many stars.

mil · lion (mil′yən) *n.* one thousand times one thousand; 1,000,000.

min · er · al (min′ər əl) *n.* a substance found in nature that is not an animal or a plant. Salt, gold, and iron are minerals.

mole (mōl) *n.* **1.** a small animal that lives underground. **2.** a brownish spot on the skin.

mon · ster (mon′stər) *n.* an imaginary creature that is huge and frightening.

Ms. (miz, em′es′) an abbreviation used as a title before a woman's name.

mu · se · um (myo͞o zē′əm) *n.* a building where objects of art, science, or history are kept.

mys · ter · y (mis′tər ē) *n.* something that is not or cannot be known, explained, or understood.

N

nar · whal (när′wəl) *n.* a small toothed whale native to Arctic seas.

nat · u · ral · ly (nach′ər ə lē) *adv.* **1.** as would be expected; of course. **2.** in a normal manner.

na · ture (nā′chər) *n.* the physical universe; all the things that are not made by people.

neigh · bor (nā′bər) *n.* a person who lives in a house or apartment next to or near one's own.

nei · ther (nē′thər, nī′thər) *conj.* nor; nor yet; no more.

net (net) *n.* an open fabric that is made of threads, cords, or ropes.

no · tice (nō′tis) *v.* **no · ticed, no · tic · ing.** to become aware of; observe.

No · vem · ber (nō vem′bər) *n.* the eleventh month of the year.

O

oc · to · pus (ok′tə pəs) *n.* an animal that lives in salt water and has a soft, round body and eight arms.

on · ion (un′yən) *n.* the round or oval bulb of a plant eaten as a vegetable. Onions have a strong, sharp taste and smell.

or · ange (ôr′inj, or′inj) *n.* a red-dish-yellow color.—*adj.* having the color orange; reddish-yellow.

P

pace (pās) *n.* **1.** a single step. **2.** the length of a single step. **3.** the rate of speed in walking.

pa · ja · mas (pə jä′məz, pə jam′əz) *n. pl.* a set of clothes to sleep in.

pan · to · mime (pan′tə mīm′) *n.* **1.** the telling of a story without talking, through the use of gestures, body movements, and facial expressions. **2.** a play acted in this way.

pars · ley (pärs′lē) *n.* a small plant that has many tiny leaves on each branch. It is used to flavor and decorate food.

pas de chat (pä′ də shä′) *n.* a cat-like leap in ballet.

pas · sage · way (pas′ij wā′) *n.* a way along which a person or thing can pass.

paste (pāst) *n.* a mixture, usually made of flour and water, used to stick things together.—*v.* **past · ed, past · ing.** to stick with paste.

ped · dler (ped′lər) *n.* a person who travels around selling goods that he or she carries from place to place.

pi · o · neer (pī′ə nēr′) *n.* a person who is the first to explore and settle a region.

pit · y (pit′ē) *n.* a feeling of sorrow and sympathy.

plan · et (plan′it) *n.* one of the nine large bodies that move around the sun. The planets are Mercury, Venus, Earth, Mars, Jupiter, Saturn, Uranus, Neptune, and Pluto.

pos · se (pos′ē) *n.* a group of men and women gathered by a sheriff to help him or her capture a criminal.

pot · ter · y (pot′ə rē) *n.* pots, bowls, dishes, and other things made from clay and hardened by heat.

pres · i · dent (prez′ə dənt) *n.* a person who is in charge; head.

pres · sure (presh′ər) *n.* force caused by one thing pushing against another.

pro · tect (prə tekt′) *v.* defend.

Pueb · lo (pweb′lō) a member of an American Indian tribe such as the Zuni or Hopi.

R

re · ceive (ri sēv′) *v.* **re · ceived, re · ceiv · ing.** to take or get something.

rec · og · nize (rek′əg nīz′) *v.* **rec · og · nized, rec · og · niz · ing.** to know that you have seen or heard about a person or thing before.

rec · ord (rek′ərd) *n.* a disk on which music or other sounds have been recorded to be played back on a phonograph.

re · cord · er (ri kôr′dər) *n.* a musical instrument that is something like a flute.

re · main (ri mān′) *v.* to stay behind or in the same place.

re · pair (ri per′) *n.* the act of fixing or putting into good condition again.

res · tau · rant (res′tər ənt) *n.* a place where food is prepared and served to customers at tables by a waiter or waitress.

rhi · noc · er · os (rī nos′ər əs) *n.* a very large animal having a thick skin and one or two horns growing on its snout. Rhinoceroses are found in Africa and Asia.

rock · et (rok′it) *n.* a device that is driven forward by a stream of hot gases. Rockets are used as fireworks and weapons and to propel spacecraft.

rus · tler (rus′lər) *n.* a cattle thief.

S

Sat · ur · day (sat′ər dē, sat′ər dā′) *n.* the seventh day of the week.

sau · cer (sô′ sər) *n.* **1.** a small shallow dish that is used for holding a cup. **2.** any similar dish, plate, or the like.

save (sāv) *v.* **saved, sav · ing. 1.** to keep or free from harm; make safe. **2.** to keep from being lost, spent, or damaged; preserve.

---

a bad, ā cake, ä father; e pet, ē me; i it, ī ice; o hot, ō open, ô off; oo wood, o͞o food; oi oil, ou out; th thin, th that; u cup, ur turn, yo͞o music; zh treasure; ə ago, taken, pencil, lemon, helpful

scarce (skārs) *adj.* difficult to get or find.

Scar·lat·ti (skär lä′tē) an Italian who wrote music.

school (skool) *n.* a large group of fish or water animals swimming together.

scis·sors (siz′ərz) *n. pl.* a tool used for cutting. Scissors have two blades that are held together in the middle. When the blades are closed, they form a double cutting edge.

scrape (skrāp) *v.* **scraped, scrap·ing. 1.** to injure or scratch by rubbing against something sharp or rough. **2.** to rub or move with a harsh, grating sound.

sea horse (sē′ hôrs′) a kind of fish with a head that looks like that of a horse.

ser·vant (sur′vənt) *n.* a person hired to do certain duties.

set·tle (set′əl) *v.* **set·tled, set·tling. 1.** to agree; decide. **2.** to make a home in a place.

Seu·rat, Georges (sə rä′, zhôrzh) a French painter.

sev·er·al (sev′ər əl) *adj.* more than two, but not many.

shoul·der (shōl′dər) *n.* the part on either side of the body to which the arms are attached.

since (sins) *adv.* from then till now.

sleuth (slooth) *n.* a detective or investigator.

smooth (smooth) *adj.* having a surface that is not uneven or rough.

split (split) *n.* **1.** a break or division in something. **2.** an exercise in which a person lets his or her body slide to the floor with the legs spread in opposite directions.

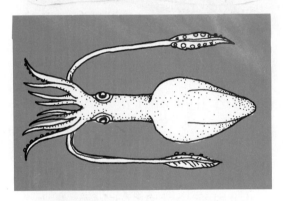

squid (skwid) *n.* an animal that is like an octopus and lives in the sea.

sug·gest (səg jest′) *v.* to offer as something to think about.

su·per (soo′pər) *n.* short for "superintendent," a person who directs or manages something.

sup·pose (sə pōz′) *v.* **sup·posed, sup·pos·ing. 1.** to imagine to be possible. **2.** to believe. **3.** to expect or require.

sus·pect (sus′pekt′) *n.* a person who is thought to be guilty.

T

tail (tāl) *v.* to follow closely.

tan · gle (tāng′gəl) *v.* **tan · gled, tan · gling.** to twist together in a confused mass; snarl.

tear (ter) *v.* **tore, torn, tear · ing.** to pull or become pulled apart.

tel · e · vi · sion (tel′ə vizh′ən) *n.* **1.** a system for sending and receiving pictures and sound over long distances. **2.** a set or device on which these pictures are seen and the sound is heard.

ter · ri · ble (ter′ə bəl) *adj.* **1.** causing fear or terror; awful. **2.** very bad.

they'd (th̲ād) contraction of "they had" and "they would."

throne (thrōn) *n.* the chair that a king or queen sits on during special occasions.

thou · sand (thou′zənd) *n.* ten times a hundred; 1,000.—*adj.* amounting to 1,000 in number.

thun · der · storm (thun′dər stôrm′) *n.* a storm that has thunder and lightning.

tore see **tear.**

to · ward (tə wôrd′, tôrd) *prep.* in the direction of.

treat · ment (trēt′mənt) *n.* the way someone or something is treated.

truth (trōōth) *n.* **1.** something that is true. **2.** the quality of being true, honest, or sincere.

twen · ty-six (twen′tē six′) *n.* a number, twenty plus six; 26.—*adj.* amounting to 26 in number.

twi · light (twī′līt′) *n.* the time just after sunset or just before sunrise.

twin (twin) *n.* one of two children or animals born at the same time to the same mother.

type · writ · er (tīp′rī′tər) *n.* a machine that prints letters.

U

un · in · ter · est · ing (un in′tə res′ting, un in′tris ting) *adj.* not causing or holding interest or attention.

---

a bad, ā cake, ä father; e pet, ē me; i it, ī ice; o hot, ō open, ô off; oo wood, ōō food; oi oil, ou out; th thin, th̲ that; u cup, ur turn, yōō music; zh treasure; ə ago, taken, pencil, lemon, helpful

un·mus·i·cal (un myoo′zi kəl) *adj.* not fond of or skilled in music.

un·u·su·al (un yoo′zhoo əl) *adj.* not usual, common, or ordinary.

V

veg·e·ta·ble (vej′ə tə bəl, vej′tə bəl) *n.* a plant whose roots, leaves, or other parts are used for food.

veil (vāl) *n.* a very thin material that is worn by women over the head or shoulders.

vi·o·la da gam·ba (vē ō′lə də gäm′bə) *n.* a stringed instrument something like a violin.

vis·i·tor (viz′i tər) *n.* a person who visits; guest.

vol·ca·no (vol kā′no) *n.* an opening in the surface of the earth through which lava, gases, and ashes are forced out.

W

wa·ter·proof (wô′tər proof′) *adj.* not letting water pass through.

wear (wer) *v.* **wore, worn, wear·ing.** to carry or have on the body.

whis·tle (hwis′əl) *v.* **whis·tled, whis·tling. 1.** to make a clear, sharp sound by forcing air out through closed lips or the teeth. **2.** to make or move with a sound like this.

whom (hoom) *pron.* the objective case of *who*.

wore (wôr) see **wear**.

write (rīt) *v.* **wrote, writ·ten, writing.** to form letters, words, or symbols of something on paper or some other surface.

writ·ten (rit′ən) see **write**.

Y

yawn (yôn) *v.* to open the mouth wide and take a deep breath.

you'd (yood) contraction of "you had" and "you would."